CONFEDERACY 101

❦ THE LOCHLAINN SEABROOK COLLECTION ❧

Everything You Were Taught About the Civil War is Wrong, Ask a Southerner!
Everything You Were Taught About American Slavery is Wrong, Ask a Southerner!
Give This Book to a Yankee! A Southern Guide to the Civil War For Northerners
Honest Jeff and Dishonest Abe: A Southern Children's Guide to the Civil War
Confederacy 101: Amazing Facts You Never Knew About America's Oldest Political Tradition
Slavery 101: Amazing Facts You Never Knew About America's "Peculiar Institution"
The Great Yankee Coverup: What the North Doesn't Want You to Know About Lincoln's War!
Confederate Blood and Treasure: An Interview With Lochlainn Seabrook
Confederate Flag Facts
A Rebel Born: A Defense of Nathan Bedford Forrest - Confederate General, American Legend (winner of the 2011 Jefferson Davis Historical Gold Medal)
A Rebel Born: The Screenplay
Nathan Bedford Forrest: Southern Hero, American Patriot - Honoring a Confederate Icon and the Old South
The Quotable Nathan Bedford Forrest: Selections From the Writings and Speeches of the Confederacy's Most Brilliant Cavalryman
Give 'Em Hell Boys! The Complete Military Correspondence of Nathan Bedford Forrest
Forrest! 99 Reasons to Love Nathan Bedford Forrest
Saddle, Sword, and Gun: A Biography of Nathan Bedford Forrest For Teens
Nathan Bedford Forrest and the Battle of Fort Pillow: The True Story
The Quotable Jefferson Davis: Selections From the Writings and Speeches of the Confederacy's First President
The Quotable Alexander H. Stephens: Selections From the Writings and Speeches of the Confederacy's First Vice President
The Alexander H. Stephens Reader: Excerpts From the Works of a Confederate Founding Father
The Quotable Robert E. Lee: Selections From the Writings and Speeches of the South's Most Beloved Civil War General
The Old Rebel: Robert E. Lee As He Was Seen By His Contemporaries
The Articles of Confederation Explained: A Clause-by-Clause Study of America's First Constitution
The Constitution of the Confederate States of America Explained: A Clause-by-Clause Study of the South's Magna Carta
The Quotable Stonewall Jackson: Selections From the Writings and Speeches of the South's Most Famous General
Abraham Lincoln: The Southern View - Demythologizing America's Sixteenth President
The Unquotable Abraham Lincoln: The President's Quotes They Don't Want You To Know!
Lincolnology: The Real Abraham Lincoln Revealed in His Own Words - A Study of Lincoln's Suppressed, Misinterpreted, and Forgotten Writings and Speeches
The Great Impersonator! 99 Reasons to Dislike Abraham Lincoln
The Quotable Edward A. Pollard: Selections From the Writings of the Confederacy's Greatest Defender
Encyclopedia of the Battle of Franklin - A Comprehensive Guide to the Conflict that Changed the Civil War
Carnton Plantation Ghost Stories: True Tales of the Unexplained from Tennessee's Most Haunted Civil War House!
The McGavocks of Carnton Plantation: A Southern History - Celebrating One of Dixie's Most Noble Confederate Families and Their Tennessee Home
Jesus and the Law of Attraction: The Bible-Based Guide to Creating Perfect Health, Wealth, and Happiness Following Christ's Simple Formula
The Bible and the Law of Attraction: 99 Teachings of Jesus, the Apostles, and the Prophets
Christ Is All and In All: Rediscovering Your Divine Nature and the Kingdom Within
Jesus and the Gospel of Q: Christ's Pre-Christian Teachings As Recorded in the New Testament
Seabrook's Bible Dictionary of Traditional and Mystical Christian Doctrines
The Way of Holiness: The Story of Religion and Myth From the Cave Bear Cult to Christianity
Christmas Before Christianity: How the Birthday of the "Sun" Became the Birthday of the "Son"
Britannia Rules: Goddess-Worship in Ancient Anglo-Celtic Society - An Academic Look at the United Kingdom's Matricentric Spiritual Past
The Book of Kelle: An Introduction to Goddess-Worship and the Great Celtic Mother-Goddess Kelle, Original Blessed Lady of Ireland
The Goddess Dictionary of Words and Phrases: Introducing a New Core Vocabulary for the Women's Spirituality Movement
Princess Diana: Modern Day Moon-Goddess - A Psychoanalytical and Mythological Look at Diana Spencer's Life, Marriage, and Death (with Dr. Jane Goldberg)
Aphrodite's Trade: The Hidden History of Prostitution Unveiled
UFOs and Aliens: The Complete Guidebook
The Caudills: An Etymological, Ethnological, and Genealogical Study - Exploring the Name and National Origins of a European-American Family
The Blakeneys: An Etymological, Ethnological, and Genealogical Study - Uncovering the Mysterious Origins of the Blakeney Family and Name

Five-Star Books & Gifts With Five-Star Service!

SeaRavenPress.com

CONFEDERACY
101

AMAZING FACTS YOU NEVER KNEW ABOUT AMERICA'S OLDEST POLITICAL TRADITION

LOCHLAINN SEABROOK

JEFFERSON DAVIS HISTORICAL GOLD MEDAL WINNER

ILLUSTRATED

SEA RAVEN PRESS, NASHVILLE, TENNESSEE, USA

CONFEDERACY 101

Published by
Sea Raven Press, Cassidy Ravensdale, President
PO Box 1484, Spring Hill, Tennessee 37174-1484 USA
SeaRavenPress.com • searavenpress@gmail.com

Sea Raven Press

Enlightening, educational, & entertaining books for the whole family!

First Sea Raven Press edition: January 2015
ISBN: 978-0-9913779-4-7
Library of Congress Control Number: 2015930135

Confederacy 101: Amazing Facts You Never Knew About America's Oldest
Political Tradition, by Lochlainn Seabrook. Includes an index, endnotes, and
bibliographical references.

Front and back cover design and art, book design, layout, and interior art by Lochlainn Seabrook
Typography: Sea Raven Press Book Design
All images, graphic design, graphic art, and illustrations copyright © Lochlainn Seabrook
Portions of this book have been adapted from the author's other works

The views on the American "Civil War" documented in this book *are* those of the publisher.

The paper used in this book is acid-free and lignin-free. It has been certified by the Sustainable Forestry
Initiative and the Forest Stewardship Council and meets all ANSI standards for archival quality paper.

PRINTED & MANUFACTURED IN OCCUPIED TENNESSEE, FORMER CONFEDERATE STATES OF AMERICA

DEDICATION

To the Confederacy and all that she stands for:
Conservative American values, traditional Southern culture,
Jeffersonianism, constitutionalism, & personal liberty.

EPIGRAPH

*"The style of the confederacy shall be,
the United States of America."*

ARTICLE ONE OF THE ARTICLES OF CONFEDERATION
NOVEMBER 15, 1777

CONTENTS

Notes to the Reader - 8
Introduction, by Lochlainn Seabrook - 9

Fact 1 - 11
Fact 2 - 12
Fact 3 - 13
Fact 4 - 14
Fact 5 - 15
Fact 6 - 16
Fact 7 - 17
Fact 8 - 18
Fact 9 - 19
Fact 10 - 20
Fact 11 - 21
Fact 12 - 22
Fact 13 - 23
Fact 14 - 25
Fact 15 - 26
Fact 16 - 27
Fact 17 - 28
Fact 18 - 30
Fact 19 - 31
Fact 20 - 32
Fact 21 - 33

Fact 22 - 34
Fact 23 - 35
Fact 24 - 36
Fact 25 - 37
Fact 26 - 38
Fact 27 - 39
Fact 28 - 41
Fact 29 - 43
Fact 30 - 44
Fact 31 - 45
Fact 32 - 46
Fact 33 - 47
Fact 34 - 48
Fact 35 - 49
Fact 36 - 50
Fact 37 - 51
Fact 38 - 52
Fact 39 - 54
Fact 40 - 55
Fact 41 - 56
Fact 42 - 57

Fact 43 - 58
Fact 44 - 59
Fact 45 - 60
Fact 46 - 61
Fact 47 - 62
Fact 48 - 63
Fact 49 - 65
Fact 50 - 66
Fact 51 - 67
Fact 52 - 68
Fact 53 - 70
Fact 54 - 71
Fact 55 - 72
Fact 56 - 73
Fact 57 - 75
Fact 58 - 77
Fact 59 - 78
Fact 60 - 79
Fact 61 - 80
Fact 62 - 81
Fact 63 - 82

Fact 64 - 83
Fact 65 - 84
Fact 66 - 85
Fact 67 - 87
Fact 68 - 89
Fact 69 - 90
Fact 70 - 91
Fact 71 - 92
Fact 72 - 93
Fact 73 - 94
Fact 74 - 95
Fact 75 - 96
Fact 76 - 97
Fact 77 - 98
Fact 78 - 99
Fact 79 - 100
Fact 80 - 101
Fact 81 - 102
Fact 82 - 103
Fact 83 - 104
Fact 84 - 105

Appendix, "The Confederacy," by Baron de Montesquieu - 108
Notes - 110
Bibliography - 116
Index - 122
Meet the Author - 125

NOTES TO THE READER

☛ In any study of America's antebellum, bellum, and postbellum periods, it is vitally important to understand that in 1860 the two major political parties—the Democrats and the newly formed Republicans—were the opposite of what they are today. In other words, the Democrats of the mid 19th Century were Conservatives, akin to the Republican Party of today, while the Republicans of the mid 19th Century were Liberals, akin to the Democratic Party of today. Thus the Confederacy's Democratic president, Jefferson Davis, was a Conservative (with libertarian leanings); the Union's Republican president, Abraham Lincoln, was a Liberal (with socialistic leanings).

☛ As I heartily dislike the phrase "Civil War," its use throughout this book (as well as in my other works) deserves an explanation.

Today America's entire literary system refers to the conflict of 1861 using the Northern term the "Civil War," whether we in the South like it or not. Thus, as *all* book searches by readers, libraries, and retail outlets are now performed online, and as *all* bookstores categorize works from this period under the heading "Civil War," book publishers and authors who deal with this particular topic have little choice but to use this term themselves. If I were to refuse to use it, as some of my Southern colleagues have suggested, few people would ever find or read my books.

Add to this the fact that scarcely any non-Southerners have ever heard of the names we in the South use for the conflict, such as the "War for Southern Independence"—or my personal preference, "Lincoln's War." It only makes sense then to use the term "Civil War" in most commercial situations.

We should also bear in mind that while today educated persons, particularly educated Southerners, all share an abhorrence for the phrase "Civil War," it was not always so. Confederates who lived through and even fought in the conflict regularly used the term throughout the 1860s, and even long after. Among them were Confederate generals such as Nathan Bedford Forrest, Richard Taylor, and Joseph E. Johnston, not to mention the Confederacy's vice president, Alexander H. Stephens. Even the Confederacy's highest leader, President Jefferson Davis, used the term "Civil War,"[1] and in one case at least, as late as 1881—the year he wrote his brilliant exposition, *The Rise and Fall of the Confederate Government*.[2]

☛ Lincoln's War on the American people and the Constitution can never be fully understood without a thorough knowledge of the South's perspective of the conflict. For those seeking to learn the *whole* truth about the "Civil War," see my books, listed on page 2.

INTRODUCTION

Preserving the Truth About
Conservatism & the Confederacy

Thanks to the industrious and villainous efforts of anti-South writers, historians, and partisans, the facts about the Confederacy have been buried beneath a mountain of slander, lies, mythology, fraud, misinformation, and patent disinformation.

As most anti-South individuals are Liberals, it is understandable that they would strongly dislike the idea of confederation, with its Jeffersonian emphasis on state sovereignty, states' rights, the rights of accession and secession, and a small limited federal government. But to distort history and mislead the public, either intentionally or out of malice or even ignorance, is inexcusable and an educational crime of unparalleled proportion. Thankfully revisionist history is always eventually found out and corrected—as it is here.

Though confederation is certainly one of the most interesting, practical, natural, attractive, ergonomic, and efficient forms of government ever formulated by the mind of man, few political ideas have ever been so widely misunderstood and criticized. In *Confederacy 101: Amazing Facts You Never Knew About America's Oldest Political Tradition*, I seek to reestablish the truth about the concept of confederation. It was the Founding Fathers' original government of choice, after all, and thus it is every American's responsibility to have, at the very least, a basic understanding of it.[3]

As the Conservative U.S. Founders and the Southern Confederate Founders well understood, it is in the preservation of the concept of confederation that we find both the last great hope of personal liberty and our only protection against government enslavement. May this little book assist in that effort.

Lochlainn Seabrook
Nashville, Tennessee, USA
January 2015

FACT 1

The Word Confederacy
Means a "Joint Compact"

The modern English word confederacy dates from the 14th Century and derives from the Anglo-French word *confederacie*, meaning a "league" or a "union."

The Anglo-French word *confederacie* derives from the Middle English word *confederat*, which derives from the Late Latin word *confoederatus*, which is the past participle of *confoederare*, meaning "to unite by a league."

The Late Latin word *confoederare* derives from the Latin word *comfoeder*, which is combination of the Latin words *com* (in certain cases spelled *con*) and *foeder*.

The Latin prefix *com* means "with," "jointly," or "together."

The Latin word *foeder* derives from the Latin *foedus*, meaning a "compact" (that is, *com* and *pact*) a word which itself means: 1) "an assemblage of separate parts joined together." 2) "a pact, contract, or agreement between two or more parties."

In its most elemental original form then, confederacy means: "joint" (*com*) "compact" (*foedus*).

Thus the original meaning of *comfoeder, confoederare, confoederatus, confederat, confederacie*, that is, confederacy, was simply: "a body of persons, states, or nations united by a league."

FACT 2

CONFEDERATION & FEDERATION
ONCE SHARED THE SAME MEANING

As the word federation derives from the word confederation, from the Latin *foedus* ("compact"), originally both confederation and federation meant the same thing.

In fact, federation was coined around the year 1721 as an abbreviation of confederation. This is why many of the Founding Fathers used the two words interchangeably, just as Alexander Hamilton did in *The Federalist* in 1788.[4]

Thus prior to the formation of the United States of America in 1776—and even for some time thereafter—confederation and federation had a single meaning: "a league of colonies or states."

Title page of a 1901 edition of *The Federalist*.

FACT 3

AMERICA HAS HAD MANY CONFEDERACIES

America has a long history of confederation and confederacies, one that dates back into prehistory among native peoples. One of the earliest known was the Aztec Confederation, which arose around the 12th Century.[5] Others were the Algonquian Confederacy, Abnaki Confederacy, Pennacook Confederacy, Blackfoot Confederacy, Caddo Confederacy, Arikara Confederacy, Creek Confederacy, Pawnee Confederacy, Utina Confederacy, Natchez Confederacy, Taensa Confederacy, Clusa Confederacy, Wappinger Confederacy, Massachuset Confederacy, Sauk Confederacy, and the Mahican Confederacy.[6]

The most familiar of the many Native-American confederacies, however, was the great Iroquois Confederacy, a well organized league formed in the late 1500s. Called the "Five Nations" by the English, the original tribes were: the Mohawk, Oneida, Seneca, Cayuga, and Onondaga. In 1722 another nation, the Tuscarora, joined, after which the Iroquois Confederacy became known as the "Six Nations."[7]

In his writings, Thomas Jefferson, a confederate scholar of note, made mention of the Powhatan Confederacy, the Maffawomee Confederacy, the Manahoack Confederacy, the Delaware Confederacy, and the Mingo (Iroquois) Confederacy.[8] Of this last Indian confederation, Elbridge S. Brooks writes:

> The confederacy thus formed by these five kindred tribes was based on the principle of absolute and fraternal equality. Each tribe remained independent so far as local self-government was concerned, but in matters of mutual interest they were united and patriotic.[9]

This same political concept, confederation, would soon be adopted by the American colonists as their preferred "style" of government.

FACT 4

THE AMERICAN COLONISTS
INTENTIONALLY FORMED A CONFEDERACY

With the issuance of the Declaration of Independence and the start of the American Revolutionary War in 1776 (inaugurating America's severance from England), the original 13 colonies set about forming a government of their own. After much debate the form of government chosen was a confederacy, or a "Confederate Republic," as Alexander Hamilton called it.[10]

Alexander Hamilton.

FACT 5

THE FIRST U.S. CONFEDERACY
WAS A NEW FORM OF GOVERNMENT

In essence the first U.S. Confederacy was a purely unique, European-American form of government, one comprised of ideas that the Founding Fathers borrowed from not only the ideas of earlier political scholars, like Baron de Montesquieu, but also real Old World confederations, such as the famed Greek confederacies that dated back to the 4th Century B.C.

The personal papers of American Founder James Madison, for example, reveal that he studied and was very familiar with the "Achaean Confederacy," the "Belgic Confederacy," the "Amphictyonic Confederacy," the "Lycian Confederacy," the "German Confederacy," the "Dutch Confederacy," and the "Swiss Confederacy,"[11] founded in 1291.[12] As noted, the writings of American Founder Thomas Jefferson show that he was a keen student of the many early Native-American Confederacies.[13]

Baron de Montesquieu.

Like many of both early Indian and European confederacies, the original U.S. Confederacy was defined as a body of states united to form a loose "association," in which the states retain all sovereign power, while the central government is legally dependent on the will of the states.[14]

At this particular time in American history, the words confederation and federation still carried the same meaning: "a league of colonies or states."

FACT 6

LIKE 18ᵗʰ-CENTURY NATIVE-AMERICANS 18ᵗʰ-CENTURY EUROPEAN-AMERICANS WERE CONFEDERATES

O n March 1, 1781, the 13 original American colonies ratified their first constitution. As the new republic was a confederacy, they called this document the "Articles of Confederation."

On this same day the Continental Congress became the "Confederate Congress" and Continental Congressmen became "Confederate Congressmen." The union of the first "Confederate States of America" was born.

Patterned on ancient and Medieval European confederacies, and quite probably Native-American confederacies as well, under their new confederate government all Americans were now literally confederates, living in a confederacy under a one-of-a-kind confederated political organization known to the Founders as a "confederate republic."[15]

Members of the Iroquois Confederacy.

FACT 7

THE FOUNDING FATHERS
CAREFULLY DEFINED "CONFEDERACY"

T he Articles of Confederation stipulated that the individual states were allowed to keep every power "which is not by this confederation expressly delegated to the United States."

This formally defined the word confederacy as it was first used by the Founding Fathers: a small, weak, decentralized government supported by a voluntary group of strong and wholly independent nation-states, whose power, authority, and sovereignty rests on the bedrock of the separation of powers, the right of secession, and states' rights.

Indeed, in 1788 in *The Federalist*, John Jay refers to the separate American colonies or states as "distinct nations."[16] In other words, the Founding Generation considered them to be autonomous nation-states,[17] wholly independent of one another,[18] each one a sovereign country and an individual government in its own right.[19]

John Jay.

FACT 8

THE FOUNDING GENERATION
CREATED A CONFEDERATE REPUBLIC

Under confederation the colonists were able to avoid their greatest fear: the formation of a single monolithic *nation*, with all of its autocratic, dictatorial overtones, enslavement under monarchical rule, political corruption, and dearth of personal freedom.

In place of a nation they very purposefully chose to form a "firm league of friendship" with one another; that is, a *confederacy*. The Confederacy in turn operated under the auspices of a republican form of government, a political body based on laws (rather than majority rule, as in a democracy) in which the supreme power lay with the people rather than with their political leaders.[20] This was, in essence, the "Confederate Republic" intended by the Founders,[21] one that served a very specific purpose, as Hamilton noted:

> It appears that the very structure of the confederacy affords the surest preventatives from error, and the most powerful checks to misconduct.[22]

Buckingham Palace, London, England, seat of the much reviled British monarchy, which early Americans viewed as a dictatorship.

FACT 9

JEFFERSON EXPECTED THE U.S.
TO BE A "LASTING CONFEDERACY"

In his notes on America's first constitution, the Articles of Confederation, Thomas Jefferson wrote of the importance of forming a confederacy:

> All men admit that a confederacy is necessary. Should the idea get abroad that there is likely to be no union among us, it will damp the minds of the people, diminish the glory of our struggle, and lessen its importance; because it will open to our view future prospects of war and dissension among ourselves. If an equal vote be refused, the smaller states will become vassals to the larger; and all experience has shown that the vassals and subjects of free states are the most enslaved.[23]

Jefferson then expressed his hope that "in the present enlightened state of men's minds we might expect a lasting confederacy . . ."[24] Here we have the great wish of one of America's most important Founding Fathers, *that the U.S. would exist forever as a confederacy.*

Thomas Jefferson.

FACT 10

THE PHRASE "PERPETUAL UNION" IS COMMONLY MISUNDERSTOOD BY YANKEES

The opening paragraphs of the Articles of Confederation refer to a "perpetual union" between the separate states, a term long misunderstood and thus misinterpreted in the North.

The word "perpetual" here was not intended to mean that a state could not leave (secede from) the U.S. Confederacy. Merely that *the union of states itself* would continue indefinitely, regardless of how many states decided to join or leave—and when, how, or why. This is a vitally important distinction.

Indeed, under the U.S. Constitution both accession and secession have always been regarded as legal states' rights, and they remain so to this day, as the 9th and 10th Amendments tacitly attest.[25]

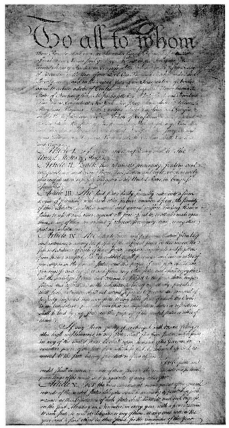

Opening paragraphs of the Articles of Confederation.

FACT 11

ORIGINALLY THE UNITED STATES OF AMERICA WAS CALLED "THE CONFEDERACY"

Though the Articles of Confederation of 1781 referred to the new republic as "the United States of America," few at the time actually called it by that name. To most it was, as Thomas Jefferson fondly referred to it, "our Confederacy,"[26] "our Confederation,"[27] "the Confederation,"[28] or more commonly "the Confederacy."[29]

Article 1 of the Articles themselves refers to the United States of America as "the Confederacy."[30] This was the name given to the original

Formulation of the Articles of Confederation.

U.S. at its founding, during the Confederate period (1781 to 1789), and even long after the Articles of Confederation were replaced in 1789 with our second constitution, the Constitution of the United States of America.

This shows, as nothing else does, that even though the country began to move toward federation and away from confederation after 1789, the U.S. was still considered a confederacy, with all that which was implied by confederation; that is, all-powerful sovereign states functioning under a weak limited national government.

FACT 12

THE U.S. CONFEDERACY LAID THE GROUNDWORK FOR THE MODERN U.S.A.

Most mainstream historians today ignore the American Confederacy, which endured from 1781 to 1789, viewing it as an unimportant era in U.S. history. However, it was not unimportant to the Founders.

Indeed, the period of colonial confederation laid the foundation for the modern United States of America, which would not exist today had it not been for this bold, early political experiment.

The Capitol Building, Washington, D.C.

FACT 13

PRIOR TO GEORGE WASHINGTON AMERICA HAD TEN CONFEDERATE PRESIDENTS

The U.S. Confederacy was a legitimate republic, with all of the rights, powers, functions, and leaders of a confederacy, including a chief executive. In all, there were ten U.S. confederate presidents who held that office prior to George Washington—our first president under the later emerging U.S. Constitution.

The first president of the U.S. under the Articles of Confederation was Samuel Huntington of Connecticut, who served from September 28, 1779 to July 6, 1781. Though it was officially known as "President of the United States in Congress Assembled," the position was that of a true *confederate* chief executive.

Samuel Huntington.

What follows is a complete list of our first ten presidents and the dates they served. Note that under the Articles of Confederation there was no executive branch, making the office of "President of the Confederate Congress" far less onerous and rigorous than that of a modern U.S. president. As specified in Article 9 of the Articles of Confederation, each presidential term was limited to one year.[31] Several men served partial terms, otherwise there would have only been eight presidents:

1. America's First Confederate President: Samuel Huntington of Connecticut (1731-1796): served from September 28, 1779, to July 6, 1781.
2. America's Second Confederate President: Thomas McKean of Delaware (1734-1817): served from July 10, 1781, to November 4, 1781.
3. America's Third Confederate President: John Hanson of Maryland (1715-1783): served from November 5, 1781, to November 4, 1782.
4. America's Fourth Confederate President: Elias Boudinot of New Jersey (1740-1821): served from November 4, 1782, to November 3, 1783.
5. America's Fifth Confederate President: Thomas Mifflin of Pennsylvania (1744-1800): served from November 3, 1783, to June 3, 1784.
6. America's Sixth Confederate President: Richard Henry Lee of Virginia (1732-1794): served from November 30, 1784, to November 23, 1785.
7. America's Seventh Confederate President: John Hancock of Massachusetts (1737-1793): served from November 23, 1785, to June 6, 1786.
8. America's Eighth Confederate President: Nathaniel Gorham of Massachusetts (1738-1796): served from June 6, 1786, to November 13, 1786.
9. America's Ninth Confederate President: Arthur St. Clair of Pennsylvania (1737-1818): served from February 2, 1787, to October 29, 1787.
10. America's Tenth Confederate President: Cyrus Griffin of Virginia (1748-1810): served from January 22, 1788, to March 4, 1789.[32]

Just two months later, on April 30, 1789, on the balcony of Federal Hall on Wall Street in New York City, Washington was sworn in as the first president of the United States of America under the newly effective U.S. Constitution. Let us now examine what became of the U.S. Confederacy (1781-1789), our first Confederate States of America, and her constitution, the Articles of Confederation.

FACT 14

EARLY LIBERALS DISLIKED THE U.S. CONFEDERACY & THE ARTICLES OF CONFEDERATION

N aturally, 18th-Century Conservatives adored the Articles of Confederation, with that document's clear and forceful accentuation of state sovereignty. But this peaceful moment in U.S. history was not to last. Liberals, of course, desired a stronger, bigger national government, and they were not about to allow a little thing like the Constitution stand in their way!

Benjamin Franklin.

In the Spring of 1781, no sooner had the ink dried on the parchment of the Articles of Confederation, than the Liberal majority (known then as the "Nationalists") began to complain about everything the Conservatives (known then as the "Federalists") liked about it.[33]

For one thing, the Nationalists argued, the articles gave Congress no power to enforce law or regulate foreign trade. Worse still, Congress could not levy state taxes. Instead, it had to ask, and in many cases literally beg, the states for money, the result being that Congress could not control the public debt. Lastly, they held, without a judiciary or an "official" president, the central government, rendered virtually "ineffective" by the articles, was unable to interpret laws, regulate commerce, or carry out the acts of Congress.[34]

FACT 15

LIBERALS SOUGHT TO OVERTHROW THE U.S. CONFEDERACY AT THE CONSTITUTIONAL CONVENTION IN 1787

By 1787 the tide had turned against the idea of a strictly confederated United States of America, and a convention was commenced at Independence Hall in Philadelphia, Pennsylvania, on May 14 of that year with the idea of *amending* the Articles of Confederation.

After much wrangling and debate, however, it soon became apparent that what the majority actually wanted was not to simply improve the articles. They desired an entirely new form of polity, one with an all-powerful, consolidated central government that had authority over the legislatures of the individual states.

The main idea put forward was that of a "supreme power," one that would simultaneously destroy the concept of state sovereignty. In short, it was at this time that Liberals began pushing for a strong nationalized government, what we now call "big government."[35]

John Adams.

FACT 16

THE U.S. CONSTITUTION UNFAIRLY
REPLACED THE ARTICLES OF CONFEDERATION

There were sporadic revolts against the plan to centralize the government, with James Madison even pointing out that the U.S. Confederacy had been "unanimously established."[36] But with the tempering voices of Thomas Jefferson, John Jay, Richard Henry Lee, John Adams, Samuel Adams, John Hancock, and Patrick Henry (who famously said "I smell a rat") absent from the proceedings (for various reasons), the U.S. Confederacy had little hope of surviving intact.

Independence Hall, Philadelphia, Pennsylvania.

The unavoidable result of the Philadelphia Convention was a brand new governing document, unjustly pushed through in 1787 by the new Liberal Party, the monarchical Federalists, led by Alexander Hamilton. Called the "Constitution of the United States of America," this, our second constitution, marked the concurrent birth of the U.S. as a true *nation*, which is defined as "a body of people [as opposed to states] belonging to and maintained by a strong, nationalized, politically organized central government."

This same year the Conservatives dropped the name "Federalists" (now taken over by Hamilton and the Liberals), and became the "Anti-Federalists" (which eventually transformed into the "Democratic-Republican Party," led by Conservative Thomas Jefferson).[37]

FACT 17

PATRICK HENRY FOUGHT TO PRESERVE THE U.S. CONFEDERACY

One of the most vociferous opponents of throwing out the Confederate Republic and turning the U.S. into a federate nation—by switching the focus from the states to "the people"—was the aforementioned fiery Conservative, Patrick Henry.

During a debate on June 4, 1788, at a convention in Richmond, Virginia, Henry made the following comments about the consequences of altering the nature of the U.S. Confederacy:

> [I am] extremely uneasy at the proposed change of government . . . . If a wrong step be made now, the republic may be lost forever. If this new government will not come up to the expectation of the people, and they shall be disappointed, their liberty will be lost, and tyranny must and will arise.

> . . . I am sure [that my Liberal colleagues are] fully impressed with the necessity of forming a great consolidated government, instead of a confederation. That this is a consolidated [big] government is demonstrably clear; and the danger of such a government is, to my mind, very striking. . . . Who authorized them to speak the language of, *We, the people*, instead of *We, the states*? States are the characteristics and the soul of a confederation. If the states be not the agents of this compact, it must be one great, consolidated, national government, of the people of all the states.

> . . . The Confederation, this same despised government [by Liberals], merits, in my opinion, the highest encomium: it carried us through a long and dangerous war; it rendered us victorious in that bloody conflict with a powerful nation; it has secured us a territory greater than any European monarch possesses: and shall a government which has been thus strong and vigorous, be accused of imbecility, and abandoned for want of energy?

Consider what you are about to do before you part with the [Confederate] government. Take longer time in reckoning things; revolutions like this have happened in almost every country in Europe; similar examples are to be found in ancient Greece and ancient Rome—instances of the people losing their liberty by their own carelessness and the ambition of a few.

We are cautioned by the honorable gentleman [Edmund Pendleton], who presides, against faction and turbulence. I acknowledge that licentiousness is dangerous, and that it ought to be provided against: I acknowledge, also, [that] the new [federal] form of government may effectually prevent it: yet there is another thing it will as effectually do—it will oppress and ruin the people.

. . . I am not well versed in history, but I will submit to your recollection whether liberty has been destroyed most often by the licentiousness of the people or by the tyranny of rulers? I imagine, sir, you will find the balance on the side of tyranny. Happy will you be if you miss the fate of those nations, who, omitting to resist their oppressors, or negligently suffering their liberty to be wrested from them, have groaned under intolerable despotism![38]

Patrick Henry.

FACT 18

AGAINST THE WISHES OF MANY OUR CONFEDERATE REPUBLIC WAS TURNED INTO A FEDERATE NATION

T he voice of reason, so eloquently and logically articulated by Conservatives like Patrick Henry, was soon drowned out. Preferring the oppressive "slavery" of life under monarchical big government to the soul-enriching individual freedoms enjoyed under confederation, the Liberals blithely trampled over both the wisdom of history and the wishes of the people.

Adopted on September 17, 1787, ratified on June 21, 1788, and made effective on March 4, 1789, the establishment of the new federal government and the U.S. Constitution marked the formal end of the American Confederation period. It had lasted only eight short years, from 1781 to 1789.

George Washington taking his oath of office in 1789.

FACT 19

THE FOUNDERS INTENDED THE U.S. TO BE A PERMANENT CONFEDERACY

However, the idea that America was created to be a "lasting confederacy"[39] did not change, and was not intended to change.[40] And it would not completely change, until a man named Abraham Lincoln entered the picture 84 years later.[41]

Americans who were forced to lived under the dictatorial tenure of socialistic Lincoln ended up voting him "the worst president" up until that time period. Indeed, it was the progressive political policies of the Liberal tyrant, whose leftist actions resulted in the near destruction of

Abraham Lincoln.

the U.S. Confederacy—as well as the cruel and unnecessary deaths of countless Americans (both North and South)—that have caused him to be abhorred throughout the traditional conservative South to this very day.[42]

FACT 20

ADAMS, HAMILTON, MADISON, JAY, & MONROE REFERRED TO THE U.S. AS "THE CONFEDERACY"

As proof that the Founders desired a permanent Confederacy, we have not only their statements, but those of various American statesmen whose words were chronicled before, during, and after the period of Confederation (1781-1789).

Samuel Adams.

Samuel Adams, for example, referred to the U.S. as a "Confederation" as early as 1776,[43] in *The Federalist* (1787-1788) Alexander Hamilton called the U.S. the "American Confederacy,"[44] while James Madison called it "the present Confederation of the American States."[45]

In the same series of essays John Jay referred to the Southern states as the "Southern Confederacy"[46] and Hamilton referred to the Northern states as the "Northern Confederacy."[47]

Like all other early American presidents and legislators, James Monroe too called the U.S. "the Confederacy" dozens if not hundreds of times throughout his writings and speeches.[48]

FACT 21

ADAMS, JEFFERSON, VAN BUREN, BENTON, TYLER, & HARRISON REFERRED TO THE U.S. AS "THE CONFEDERACY"

In 1782 John Adams labeled the U.S. "the Confederacy,"[49] while Thomas Jefferson spoke of "our confederated fabric" in 1820,[50] and was still referring to the U.S. as "our confederacy" in 1823, just three years before his death.[51] In his 1837 Inaugural Address U.S. President Martin Van Buren referred to the country as "our confederacy."[52]

Missouri Senator Thomas Hart Benton made mention of the U.S. "confederacy" in 1831[53] and again in 1844,[54] in 1836 future U.S. President John Tyler referred to his country as "the Confederacy,"[55] and in his Inaugural Address in 1841 President William H. Harrison declared that "our confederacy" is a government of "confederate states."[56]

Thomas Hart Benton.

FACT 22

POLK, DAVIS, & TOOMBS REFERRED TO THE U.S. AS "THE CONFEDERACY"

In 1845 President James Knox Polk mentioned "our Confederacy" and "our confederation" in his First Inaugural Address,[57] and in 1848 the future president of the Southern Confederacy, Jefferson Davis (named after Thomas Jefferson),[58] spoke of the U.S. as "this glorious Confederacy," just twelve years prior to Lincoln's election.[59] In 1849 Robert A. Toombs of Georgia referred to "this Confederacy" on the floor of the House.[60] And it was not just 19th-Century Southerners.

Robert A. Toombs.

FACT 23

CASS, PIERCE, & DOUGLAS REFERRED TO THE U.S. AS "THE CONFEDERACY"

Northerners too correctly called the U.S. "the Confederacy."[61] In a December 24, 1847, letter, Governor Lewis Cass of Michigan used the phrase "the people of the Confederacy,"[62] and during his First Inaugural Address in 1853 American President Franklin Pierce of New Hampshire made reference to "this Confederacy."[63] During his seventh and final debate with Lincoln on October 15, 1858, Illinois Senator Stephen A. Douglas referred to the U.S. as "a confederacy of sovereign and equal states."[64]

Franklin Pierce.

FACT 24

LINCOLN REFERRED TO THE
U.S. AS "THE CONFEDERACY"

Abraham Lincoln himself, a self-professed "northern man,"[65] labeled the nation "the Confederation" during this same debate with Douglas at Alton, Illinois, and as "the Confederacy," both during his New York address at the Cooper Institute on February 27, 1860,[66] and as president-elect during his speech at Independence Hall, Philadelphia, Pennsylvania, on February 22, 1861.[67]

Abraham Lincoln.

FACT 25

IN 1789 WASHINGTON CALLED THE U.S. "THE NEW CONFEDERACY"

E ven the U.S. Constitution of 1789 refers to our country, in its original form, as a Confederacy. Article 6 states:

> All debts contracted and engagements entered into, before the adoption of this Constitution, shall be as valid against the United States under this Constitution, as under the Confederation.[68]

It is clear that the Founding Generation continued to see the U.S. as a confederacy even after the adoption of the U.S. Constitution that year.

One of these was the country's first post-Articles chief executive, President George Washington, who referred to the newly refurbished government as "the new Confederacy." This definitively illustrates that he viewed the new governmental system under the U.S. Constitution as being identical to the old one under the Articles of Confederation.[69]

George Washington.

FACT 26

PINCKNEY, PHILLIPS, HAMILTON, & JACKSON REFERRED TO THE U.S. AS "THE CONFEDERATE STATES"

In 1787 South Carolina Governor Thomas Pinckney called the U.S.A. "the confederated states,"[70] and in 1799 Samuel Phillips, president of the Massachusetts Senate, referred to his fellow states as "confederate states."[71]

In an 1832 speech South Carolina Governor James Hamilton, Jr. spoke repeatedly of the U.S.A. as "our confederate states,"[72] and in 1833 Andrew Jackson made reference to "our confederation," calling it a union of "confederate states."[73]

Andrew Jackson.

FACT 27

EARLY AMERICANS & FOREIGNERS CALLED THE U.S. "THE CONFEDERATE STATES OF AMERICA"

Most revealing is the fact that the United States of America—which Madison called "the present Confederation of the American States"[74]—was, from the very beginning, known to both American citizens and foreigners as not only "the confederate states," but more importantly as "the Confederate States of America."

In 1779, for example, in the midst of the American Revolutionary War, and two years before the original 13 colonies were first confederated under the Articles of Confederation in 1781, Reverend David S. Rowland, Minister of the Presbyterian Church at Providence, Rhode Island, published a small book with the unwieldy title: *Historical Remarks, with Moral Reflections: A Sermon Preached at Providence, June 6, 1779, Wherein are Represented, the Remarkable Dispensations of Divine Providence to the People of these States, Particularly in the Rise and Progress of the Present War, Between the Confederate States of America, and Great-Britain.*[75]

Three years later, in 1782, an anonymous English author using the pseudonym "a Man of No Party," referred to the U.S.A. as "the confederate states of America."[76] That same year minister Robert Smith of Pequea, Pennsylvania, penned a book entitled: *The Obligations of the Confederate States of North America to Praise God.*[77] This was 79 years before the official formation of the Southern Confederacy in 1861.

A half century later, writing in the early 1830s, French aristocrat and tourist Alexis de Tocqueville made the following statements after visiting the U.S., all some 30 years prior to the formation of the Southern Confederacy:

> . . . the *confederate states of America* [that is, the United States of

America] had been long accustomed to form a portion of one empire before they had won their independence: they had not contracted the habit of governing themselves, and their national prejudices had not taken deep root in their minds. Superior to the rest of the world in political knowledge, and sharing that knowledge equally among themselves, they were little agitated by the passions which generally oppose the extension of federal authority in a nation, and those passions were checked by the wisdom of the chief citizens.[78]

The plain fact is that *all* of America's early presidents, statesmen, politicians, judicial scholars, and citizens viewed the United States as a confederate republic. This even included 18th- and 19th-Century Liberals, each who unfailingly maintained that the country was a "confederation of sovereign states." This is indeed why nearly everyone endearingly referred to the U.S.A. variously as "the Confederate States," "our Confederacy," "our Confederation," the "American Confederacy," or most accurately, "the Confederate States of America."

Alexis de Tocqueville.

FACT 28

THE ORIGINAL U.S. WAS MEANT TO BE A BODY OF "STATES UNITED" NOT "UNITED STATES"

Furthermore, during the 1789 ratification process of the new U.S. Constitution, the various colonies made it clear that the document was not "a Constitution for the United States" under *federation* (big government, minimal states' rights). It was "a Constitution for States United" under *confederation* (small government, optimal states' rights).[79] As Jefferson Davis later remarked concerning the Philadelphia Convention in 1787:

> It was as 'United States'—not as a state, or united people—that these colonies—still distinct and politically independent of each other—asserted and achieved their independence of the mother-country. As 'United States' they adopted the Articles of Confederation, in which the separate sovereignty, freedom, and independence of each was distinctly asserted. They were 'united States' when Great Britain acknowledged the absolute freedom and independence of each, distinctly and separately recognized by name. France and Spain were parties to the same treaty, and the French and Spanish idioms still express and perpetuate, more exactly than the English, the true idea intended to be embodied in the title—*les États Unis*, or *los Estados Unidos*—the States united.[80]

In other words, the Founding Fathers did not view the U.S. Confederacy as "the whole mass of the people of the states," but rather as the American states united by the original compact under confederation,[81] an important distinction.

In 1868, three years after the end of Lincoln's War, former Confederate Vice President Alexander H. Stephens wrote similarly:

> [Our government] . . . is a Government instituted by States and for States, and . . . all the functions it possesses, even in its direct action on the individual citizens of the several States, spring from

and depend upon a Compact between the States constituting it. It is, therefore, a Government of States and for States. The final action upon the very first resolution . . . shows that the object of the [Philadelphia] Convention [of 1787] was to form a Government of States. 'The Government of the United States' ought to consist, they declared, 'of a Supreme Legislature, Judiciary and Executive.' This is the same as if they had declared 'the Government of the States United, ought to consist,' etc. The first Constitution, we have seen, was a Government of States. The States in Congress assembled passed all laws, made all treaties, and exercised all powers vested in them jointly. No measure could be passed without the equal voice of each State, however small. Delaware had the same influence as New York, Massachusetts, or Virginia, and in this respect I maintain there is no essential change in the new Constitution.[82]

Alexander H. Stephens.

FACT 29

THE MEANING OF "CONFEDERATION" & "FEDERATION" CHANGED AFTER 1789

After 1789—with the replacement of the Articles of Confederation with the U.S. Constitution—the definition of the words confederation and federation, once identical in meaning, changed.

Federation came to imply a tighter union between the states with emphasis on the supremacy of the national government (similar to the German *Bundesstaat*), while confederation came to imply a loose union of self-governing states in which the sovereign independence of each state is emphasized (similar to the German *Staatenbund*). These new definitions would carry on into the Civil War period.[83]

Meeting of the Confederate or Continental Congress.

FACT 30

NEW ENGLAND, NOT THE SOUTH, WAS THE FIRST REGION TO TRY BOTH CONFEDERATION & SECESSION

One of the greatest Yankee myths is that the Southern states were the first to "rebel" by attempting to secede from the Union and institute a confederacy. The truth is that long before the formation of the Southern Confederacy in 1861, the New England states had been seriously discussing these two ideas, and were in fact the first to try both. During the early 1800s alone, New England would try at least three times to secede from the Union,[84] while Massachusetts attempted secession on four different occasions, all—it should be noted—without any resistance from the Southern states, or any other state for that matter.[85]

New England was already displaying great enthusiasm for the idea of confederation over a century before the formation of the United States of America. In 1856 historian James V. Marshall wrote of New England's first experiment with the idea, a 43 year long confederation formed in the year 1643—as was noted by, among others, Thomas Jefferson:[86]

> In 1643, the colonies of New Haven, Plymouth, Massachusetts, and Connecticut, entered into a confederacy, under the name of the United Colonies of New England, which continued till 1686. It was then stipulated that two commissioners from each colony should meet annually, to decide on matters of common concern; that the votes of six members should bind the whole; that in every war, each colony should furnish its quota of men money and provisions, in proportion to the number of people; and that every colony should be distinct, and have exclusive jurisdiction within its own territory. Though the strong members of this confederacy did not always act in a liberal manner toward their associates, yet it increased the power and security of the whole.[87]

FACT 31

THE NEW ENGLAND CONFEDERACY WAS THE PROTOTYPE UPON WHICH BOTH THE U.S. CONFEDERACY & THE SOUTHERN CONFEDERACY WERE LATER DESIGNED

On May 29, 1843, John Quincy Adams gave a speech before the Massachusetts Historical Society called "The New England Confederacy of 1643." The occasion was the "celebration of the second centennial anniversary of that event." Said Adams:

> The New England confederation originated in the Plymouth colony, and was probably suggested to them by the example which they had witnessed, and under which they had lived for several years in the United Netherlands. . . . At the formation of the New England union . . . [it] then consisted of four separate independent communities [Massachusetts, Plymouth, Connecticut, and New Haven], in a great measure self-formed; the vital principle common to them all being religious contention—and the quickening spirit, equal rights, freedom of thought and action, and personal independence. . . . [After entering] into a firm and perpetual league of friendship and amity for offence and defence, mutual advice and succor upon all just occasions . . . [they were henceforth] called by the name of *the United Colonies of New England*. . . . The New England confederacy of 1643 was the model and prototype of the North American [U.S.] confederacy of 1774. . . . Of the North American [U.S.] confederacy, self-constituted in the progress of the [American] revolution which converted the thirteen English colonies into independent states, New England forms a constituent part . . . [88]

In short, according to one of our own presidents, the New England Confederacy laid the groundwork for the creation of the U.S. Confederacy in 1781. And this was, of course, the model for the Southern Confederacy in 1861—more proof that the South did not secede to destroy the government of the Founders, but to preserve it.

FACT 32

LIBERAL NEW ENGLAND SOUGHT SECESSION OVER COMPLAINTS ABOUT THE CONSERVATIVE SOUTH

Yankee secessionist sentiment was born of infuriation over several legislative actions by then U.S. President Thomas Jefferson (who served from 1801 to 1809). These included the Louisiana Purchase (1803), the Embargo Act—which placed restrictions on Yankee merchants and exporters (1807), and the War of 1812 (caused, in part, by the embargo).

These actions, and others that were felt to negatively impact the North, launched the 14 year New England Secession Movement, led by Massachusetts Senator Timothy Pickering, George Washington's former adjutant general,[89] and later President John Adams' secretary of state.[90]

James Monroe.

FACT 33

NEW ENGLAND SECESSIONISTS
DESIRED RACIAL APARTHEID

In a March 4, 1804, letter to fellow New Englander Rufus King (like most other Yankees, both a Federalist and an advocate of black colonization),[91] Jefferson-hating Pickering discussed the proposed secession plan of the Northern states:

> I am disgusted with the [Southern] men who now rule us and with their measures. At some manifestations of their malignancy I am shocked. . . . I am therefore ready to say 'come out from among them and be ye separate.' . . . Were New York detached (as under his [Aaron Burr's] administration it would be) from the Virginian influence, the whole Union would be benefitted. [President] Jefferson would then be forced to observe some caution and forbearance in his measures. And, if a separation should be deemed proper, the five New England States, New York, and New Jersey would naturally be united. Among those seven States, there is a sufficient congeniality of character to authorize the expectation of practicable harmony and a permanent union, New York the centre. Without a separation, can those States ever rid themselves of negro Presidents and negro Congresses, and regain their just weight in the political balance? . . . As population is *in fact* no rule of taxation, the negro representation ought to be given up. If refused, it would be a strong ground of separation; tho' perhaps an earlier occasion may occur to declare it.[92]

Rufus King.

FACT 34

THE HARTFORD CONVENTION & THE NEW ENGLAND CONFEDERACY

The brewing issue finally culminated in the Hartford Convention, a secession conference held from December 15, 1814, to January 5, 1815.[93]

Here, 26 Federalist delegates (Liberals) met secretly to not only propose amendments that would lessen the influence of the South,[94] but to discuss leaving the Union in order to form a new and separate confederacy, the "New England Confederacy," as they called it, one they hoped would eventually include New York, Pennsylvania, and even Nova Scotia.[95]

Among the convention's recommendations were allowing the states in the New England Confederacy greater military control, as well as amendments to the U.S. Constitution that would limit the powers of Congress and the executive.[96]

The Hartford Convention or *LEAP NO LEAP*.

A caricature of the Hartford Convention, published in 1814.

FACT 35

THE NEW ENGLAND CONFEDERACY WAS THE FIRST TRUE CONFEDERATE REBELLION AGAINST THE UNION

The New England Confederacy was in "rebellion" from its very inception: it opposed the War of 1812 and refused to obey President James Madison's call for troops.[97] All of this took place nearly a half century before the secession of the Southern states and the formation of the Southern Confederacy in 1861.

James Madison.

FACT 36

IN 1814 YANKEES CALLED
FOR A RACIST SECESSION

A furious, anti-South Pickering—who once called Southern hero Thomas Jefferson a "revolutionary monster," and accused him of cruelty, cowardice, turpitude, corruption, and baseness[98]—spoke for all of the members of the Hartford Convention:

> I will rather anticipate a new Confederacy, exempt from the corrupt and corrupting influence of the aristocratic Democrats [Conservatives] of the South. There will be—and our children at farthest will see it—a separation. The white and black population will mark the boundary. The British Provinces, even with the assent of Britain, will become members of the Northern confederacy. A continued tyranny of the present ruling sect will precipitate that event.[99]

Timothy Pickering.

FACT 37

AT THE TIME OF THE NORTHERN CONFEDERACY THE U.S. RECOGNIZED THE RIGHT OF SECESSION

With congressional ratification of the Treaty of Ghent on February 15, 1815, the War of 1812 soon came to an end.[100] New England then decided against secession, though only for economic reasons. The important point, however, is that had she desired to do so, New England could have seceded legally and peacefully—and unlike Lincoln's violent, militaristic reaction to Southern secession, the South would not have stood in New England's way.[101]

Jefferson Davis.

Why? There was never any doubt among Americans at the time that the individual states were independent nations, and that secession was therefore a constitutional right, as Southern President Woodrow Wilson would later confirm in his writings.[102] Indeed, this is why Lincoln's predecessor, President James Buchanan, allowed the first seven Southern states to leave the Union in peace in late 1860 and early 1861.[103] As Jefferson Davis noted of America's fifteenth president:

> Like all who had intelligently and impartially studied the history of the formation of the Constitution, he held that the federal government had no rightful power to coerce a state.[104]

FACT 38

PRESIDENT JAMES BUCHANAN
ACKNOWLEDGED THE RIGHT OF SECESSION

D avis was referring to Buchanan's final annual message, which he gave on December 4, 1860, just before vacating his office to Lincoln. Unfortunately, the latter did not possess the former's firm knowledge of constitutional history, as is evident from the following excerpt from Buchanan's speech. Note that he refers to the U.S. as "the Confederacy" only five months before Lincoln's War:

The question, fairly stated, is: Has the Constitution delegated to Congress the power to coerce a State into submission which is attempting to withdraw or has actually withdrawn from the [U.S.] Confederacy? If answered in the affirmative, it must be on the principle that the power has been conferred upon Congress to declare and to make war against a State. After much serious reflection I have arrived at the conclusion that no such power has been delegated to Congress nor to any other department of the Federal Government. It is manifest, upon an inspection of the Constitution, that this is not among the specific and enumerated powers granted to Congress; and it is equally apparent that its exercise is not 'necessary and proper for carrying into execution' any one of these powers. So far from this power having been delegated to Congress, it was expressly refused by the Convention which framed the Constitution. It appears, from the proceedings of that body, that on the 31st May, 1787, the clause 'authorizing an exertion of the force of the whole against a delinquent State' came up for consideration. Mr. Madison opposed it in a brief but powerful speech, from which I shall extract but a single sentence. He observed: 'The use of force against a State would look more like a declaration of war than an infliction of punishment, and would

James Buchanan.

probably be considered by the party attacked as a dissolution of all previous compacts by which it might be bound.' Upon his motion the clause was unanimously postponed, and was never, I believe, again presented. Soon afterwards, on the 8th June, 1787, when incidentally adverting to the subject, he said: 'Any Government for the United States, formed on the supposed practicability of using force against the unconstitutional proceedings of the States, would prove as visionary and fallacious as the government of Congress,' evidently meaning the then existing Congress of the old Confederation [1781-1789].

Without descending to particulars, it may be safely asserted that the power to make war against a State is at variance with the whole spirit and intent of the Constitution. Suppose such a war should result in the conquest of a State, how are we to govern it afterwards? Shall we hold it as a province and govern it by despotic power? In the nature of things we could not, by physical force, control the will of the people, and compel them to elect Senators and Representatives to Congress, and to perform all the other duties depending upon their own volition, and required from the free citizens of a free State as a constituent member of the [U.S.] Confederacy.

But, if we possessed this power, would it be wise to exercise it under existing circumstances? The object would doubtless be to preserve the Union. War would not only present the most effectual means of destroying it, but would banish all hope of its peaceable reconstruction. Besides, in the fraternal conflict a vast amount of blood and treasure would be expended, rendering future reconciliation between the States impossible. In the meantime who can foretell what would be the sufferings and privations of the people during its existence?

The fact is, that our Union rests upon public opinion, and can never be cemented by the blood of its citizens shed in civil war. If it cannot live in the affections of the people, it must one day perish. Congress possesses many means of preserving it by conciliation; but the sword was not placed in their hand to preserve it by force. [105]

These brilliant utterances, verbalized by a rank-and-file Northerner, [106] were words that every Southerner could truly appreciate, and hopes were high that when Lincoln—himself originally a Southerner—entered the White House, he would follow in Buchanan's footsteps. [107]

FACT 39

ABRAHAM LINCOLN ONCE HELD SECESSION TO BE LEGAL, "SACRED," & "VALUABLE"

Secession is lawful, Lincoln once asserted! He even called it a "most sacred right." On January 12, 1848, in a speech before the U.S. House of Representatives, he declared:

> Any people anywhere, being inclined and having the power, have the right to rise up, and shake off the existing government, and form a new one that suits them better. This is a most valuable, a most sacred right—a right which, we hope and believe, is to liberate the world. Nor is this right confined to cases in which the whole people of an existing government may choose to exercise it. Any portion of such people that can may revolutionize, and make their own of so much of the territory as they inhabit.[108]

Abraham Lincoln.

FACT 40

AFTER BECOMING PRESIDENT, LIBERAL LINCOLN TURNED ANTI-SECESSIONIST

W hen it was politically expedient to change his mind, Lincoln, of course, did just that. As U.S. president 13 years later, on July 4, 1861, in his "Message to Congress in Special Session," he called the new Southern Confederacy an "illegal organization,"[109] and the constitutional right of secession an "ingenious sophism," an "insidious debauching of the public mind," and a "sugar-coated invention" of the South.[110] Those who challenged these views were labeled "traitors" and "rebels."

This is how Confederate soldiers got the epithet "Johnny Rebel," and how the name of Lincoln's War, "the War of Rebellion," came about. It is also why, after the War, Confederate officers were charged with "treason": for believing in, and acting on, the legal right of secession. Even the term Copperhead (meaning a Northerner who sympathized with the South) was anti-South: incorrectly and insultingly it likened such supporters to the deadly venomous snake of the same name.[111]

Battle of White Oak Swamp, June 30, 1862, the fifth of the Seven Days' Battles.

FACT 41

THE SOUTHERN STATES POSSESSED THE CONSTITUTIONAL RIGHT TO SECEDE

B ut Lincoln and his Northern constituents were wrong about secession. Dead wrong! Secession in the U.S. has been legal since March 1, 1781, the day our first constitution, the Articles of Confederation, was ratified into law.

How can this be, some will ask, when the right of secession does not appear anywhere in the U.S. Constitution?

While it is true that this important right is not plainly listed, there is nothing in the Constitution prohibiting it. Furthermore, it is *implied* in the Bill of Rights under the Ninth and Tenth Amendments:

NINTH AMENDMENT
The enumeration in the Constitution, of certain rights, shall not be construed to deny or disparage others retained by the people.

This amendment guarantees the American people that their power will not be taken from them by a dictatorial leader.[112]

TENTH AMENDMENT
The powers not delegated to the United States by the Constitution, nor prohibited by it to the States, are reserved to the States respectively, or to the people.

This amendment guarantees the American people that the central government cannot assume any powers which have not been assigned to it.[113]

FACT 42

THE NATIONAL GOVERNMENT DOES NOT POSSESS THE POWER TO PROHIBIT SECESSION

What are these governmental "powers"? This question is answered in what is known as the "Guarantee Clause," Article 4, Section 4, of the U.S. Constitution:

> The United States shall guarantee to every state in this union a republican form of government, and shall protect each of them against invasion; and on application of the legislature, or of the executive (when the legislature cannot be convened) against domestic violence.

In plain English, the American people have officially and constitutionally given only two powers to the U.S. federal or national government:

1. *The guarantee of a republican form of government*: each state is promised that within its own state government, the supreme power will rest with the people, not with the national government.

2. *Protection of each state against foreign and domestic invasion*: the states can expect the national government to guard them against all forms of violence from within and from without the country.

Beyond these two items the federal government possesses no rights, powers, or responsibilities. The states remain the repositories of *all* other rights, including the rights of accession and secession.

FACT 43

CONFEDERATION PRESERVES
PERSONAL LIBERTY

T he rights articulated in the Ninth and Tenth Amendments are inherent aspects of confederation: a loose, friendly coalition of powerful, self-governing, sovereign states, operating under a small, limited decentralized national government *possessing only two powers.*

According to the confederate ideals of the Founders, the central government was to deal with foreign issues, state governments with local ones. It was only by way of confederation, Confederalists or Conservatives believed, that personal liberty could be preserved.[114] After all, they had only recently fought an acrimonious and bloody war of independence against a strong central government: Britain's.[115]

Woodcut by Benjamin Franklin, published May 9, 1754, urging the British-American colonies to unite against the French. Note that the colonies are depicted as individual nation-states.

FACT 44

UNDER CONFEDERATION THE
UNION IS A VOLUNTARY COMPACT

Since the U.S. began as, and still is, a confederacy, and because a confederacy is a *voluntary* union, new territories cannot be forced to accede (enter the Union). They must accede voluntarily. It then naturally follows that they cannot be forced to remain in the Union, but have a right to secede (leave the Union) voluntarily if and when they so desire.

The U.S. Founders forging a *voluntary* confederacy in 1776.

This is a form of reasoning that a third-grader could understand. Yet it was (and still is) beyond some of the greatest minds in the North!

Indeed, many foreigners have shown a far greater understanding of the voluntary nature of the American Union—and her concomitant confederate rights of accession and secession—than our own politicians. One of these was French aristocrat Alexis de Tocqueville, who wrote the following in the early 1800s:

> The [American] Union was formed by the voluntary agreement of States; and, in uniting together, they have not forfeited their nationality, nor have they been reduced to the condition of one and the same people. If one of the States chose to withdraw its name from the contract, it would be difficult to disprove its right of doing so; and the Federal Government would have no means of maintaining its claims directly either by force or by right.[116]

FACT 45

THE RIGHT OF SECESSION WAS PURPOSEFULLY NOT MENTIONED IN THE U.S. CONSTITUTION

Why was the right of secession not clearly spelled out in the U.S. Constitution? It was so well-known and accepted at the time that the Founders did not feel it was necessary. Jefferson Davis answered the question this way:

> It was not necessary in the Constitution to affirm the right of secession, because it was an attribute of sovereignty, and the states had reserved all which they had not delegated [to the central government].[117]

Jefferson Davis.

FACT 46

THE RIGHT OF SECESSION WAS
ONCE A NATIONALLY ACCEPTED FACT

One Yankee who *did* understand the U.S. right of secession was constitutional scholar William Rawle of Pennsylvania, who, in 1829, said: "though not expressed, [it] was mutually understood."[118]

Actually, up until 1865, secession was the most frequently discussed political issue in both the United States and the Confederate States.[119] Thus to the Framers and the general populace, it was merely another common law that was universally recognized and accepted by every American citizen.

William Rawle.

FACT 47

THE CONFEDERATE RIGHT OF SECESSION HELPS PROTECT THE PEOPLE FROM FEDERAL CONSOLIDATION

In 1863, Abel Parker Upshur, a Virginia judge, lawyer, politician, and both the secretary of the navy and secretary of state under U.S. President John Tyler, wrote the following:

> [The right of secession] . . . is not found within the Constitution but exists independent of it. As that Constitution was formed by sovereign States, they alone are authorized, whenever the question arises between them and their common government, to determine, in the last resort, what powers they intended to confer on it. This is an inseparable incident of sovereignty; a right which belongs to the States, simply because they have never surrendered it to any other power. But to render this right available for any good purpose, it is indispensably necessary to maintain the States in their proper position. If their people suffer them to sink into the insignificance of mere municipal corporations, it will be vain to invoke their protection against the gigantic power of the federal government. This is the point to which the vigilance of the people should be chiefly directed. Their highest interest is at home; their palladium is their own State governments. They ought to know that they can look nowhere else with perfect assurance of safety and protection. Let them then maintain those governments, not only in their rights, but in their dignity and influence. Make it the interest of their people to serve them; an interest strong enough to resist all the temptations of federal office and patronage. Then alone will their voice be heard with respect at Washington; then alone will their interposition avail to protect their own people against the usurpations of the great central power. It is vain to hope that the federative [that is, Confederative] principle of our government can be preserved, or that any thing can prevent it from running into the absolutism of consolidation, if we suffer the rights of the States to be filched away, and their dignity and influence to be lost, through our carelessness or neglect.[120]

FACT 48

THE RIGHT OF SECESSION IS AN
INHERENT ASPECT OF CONFEDERATION

From such words of political wisdom alone, it is apparent to all thinking people that secession was legal in 1860, and that it remains a fundamental right of the fifty states to this day. Still, no matter how we choose to interpret the Constitution, it is patently obvious what the Founders' intentions were concerning this issue 225 years ago. In June 1816, the man who authored the Declaration of Independence, now former President Thomas Jefferson, wrote a letter to William Crawford that read in part:

> If any state in the Union will declare that it prefers separation to a continuance in the Union, I have no hesitation in saying, 'Let us separate.'[121]

President Jefferson Davis, named after Thomas Jefferson, and an adept student of the U.S. Constitution, noted that in addition to the Tenth Amendment, several state Constitutions openly refer to the right of secession. Virginia's Constitution, for example, affirms that

> the powers granted under the [U.S.] Constitution, being derived from the people of the United States, may be resumed by them, whensoever the same shall be perverted to their injury or oppression, and that every power not granted thereby remains with them and at their will.[122]

The Constitutions of New York and Rhode Island also include clauses regarding secession, stating that

> the powers of government may be resumed by the people whenever it shall become necessary to their happiness.[123]

As Davis points out in his extraordinary memorial to the Southern

Confederacy, *The Rise and Fall of the Confederate Government*:

> By inserting these declarations in their ordinances, Virginia, New York, and Rhode Island formally, officially, and permanently declared their interpretation of the [U.S.] Constitution as recognizing the right of secession by the resumption of their grants. By accepting the ratifications with this declaration incorporated, the other states as formally accepted the principle which it asserted. [124]

When, beginning in 1860, the South began acting on this principal, of legal, peaceful "separation" and the resumption of "the powers of government," it was derogatorily called a "rebellion" by Lincoln, as if it were unlawful and one of the greatest of political sins. [125] However, here is what Thomas Jefferson, writing from Paris, France, to James Madison on January 30, 1787, said on this subject:

> The spirit of resistance to government is so valuable on certain occasions, that I wish it always to be kept alive. It will often be exercised when wrong, but better so than not to be exercised at all. I like a little rebellion now and then. It is [cleansing,] like a storm in the atmosphere. [126]

After decades of interference from the Northern states, the South finally decided to exercise her Constitutional right to foment "a little rebellion," a Jeffersonian act of secession that was both correct and legal according to every important, official document created by the U.S. government up to that time. Let us recall President Jefferson's words from his First Inaugural Address:

> If there be any among us who would wish to dissolve this union or to change its republican form, let them stand undisturbed as monuments of the safety with which error of opinion may be tolerated where reason is left free to combat it. [127]

If any states want to secede, Jefferson noted further:

> It is the elder and the younger son differing. God bless them both, and keep them in the union, if it be for their good, but separate them, if it be better. [128]

FACT 49

THE FOUNDERS INTENDED THE SEPARATE STATES TO BE AUTONOMOUS "LITTLE REPUBLICS"

I t was from these very ideas that America's first and second Confederacies were created: the former in 1776, to "throw off" the despotic government of Britain's King George III; the latter, in 1861, to "throw off" the despotic government of America's "King Abraham."

King George III.

In both cases, the Founders' intention was to form a government in which the Union was subservient to the individual states. In 1776 this succeeded because the colonies, which were considered individual nation-states[129]—a loose union of sovereign and independent "little republics," as Jefferson styled them,[130] or "distinct nations," as Jay referred to them[131]—were the creators of the Union, not products of the Union, as Liberals wrongly claim.

FACT 50

THE AMERICAN COLONIES SECEDED
FROM BRITAIN AS SEPARATE NATIONS

This is why, in 1781, Thomas Jefferson spoke of Virginia as "but one of thirteen nations, who have agreed to act and speak together."[132] It is because of this concept, state sovereignty, that there *cannot* be a Union without states. And it is why there *can* be states without a Union, contrary to what Lincoln believed and preached.

The Boston Tea Party, December 16, 1773.

This is also why, during the First American War of Independence, the American colonies did not secede from Britain as a unified body. While independence was declared jointly, each state, a nation in its own right, declared itself independent individually.[133]

Hence, when King George III signed an agreement recognizing the nation-states known as the "original thirteen colonies" as sovereign, he addressed each one individually, by name.[134] In Article 1 of the *Treaty With Great Britain*, we find the following passage:

> His Britannic Majesty acknowledges the said United States, viz.,
> New Hampshire, Massachusetts Bay, Rhode Island and Providence
> Plantations, Connecticut, New York, New Jersey, Pennsylvania,
> Delaware, Maryland, Virginia, North Carolina, South Carolina,
> and Georgia, to be free, sovereign and independent States; that he
> treats with them as such, and for himself, his heirs and successors,
> relinquishes all claims to the Government, propriety and territorial
> rights of the same, and every part thereof.[135]

FACT 51

SOUTHERNERS PLEDGED THEIR ALLEGIANCE TO THEIR HOME STATES, NOT THE U.S.

That the original thirteen American colonies began life as separate nation-states is the same reason early Americans pledged their allegiance to their native states rather than to the U.S.[136] Hence the majority of Southerners, like Robert E. Lee, literally referred to their home states as "my country." Though admitting that he was a citizen of the United States, Jefferson Davis observed that "my allegiance is first due to the State I represent."[137]

John Randolph.

Thomas Jefferson too called Virginia "my country."[138] John Randolph of Virginia took note of the North's desire to exact allegiance from the Southern states, saying:

> When I speak of my country, I mean the Commonwealth of Virginia. I was born in allegiance to [the English King] George III.
> . . . My ancestors threw off the oppressive yoke of the mother country, but they never made me subject to New England in matters spiritual or temporal; neither do I mean to become so voluntarily.[139]

Thus in the Old South one would refer to himself as a Tennessean, a South Carolinian, a Floridian, a Virginian, or a Texan, while a Northerner would refer to himself as a "citizen of the United States."[140]

FACT 52

EARLY AMERICANS REFERRED TO THEIR COLONIES AS "FREE & INDEPENDENT STATES"

If any doubts remain as to these facts, we need only examine the last paragraph of the Declaration of Independence. In breaking their ties with Great Britain, the leaders of the 13 American colonies repeatedly refer to themselves as "Free and Independent States," each endowed with all the powers of a sovereign nation:

> We, therefore, the Representatives of the United States of America, in General Congress, Assembled, appealing to the Supreme Judge of the world for the rectitude of our intentions, do, in the Name, and by Authority of the good People of these Colonies, solemnly publish and declare, That these united Colonies are, and of Right ought to be Free and Independent States, that they are Absolved from all Allegiance to the British Crown, and that all political connection between them and the State of Great Britain, is and ought to be totally dissolved; and that as Free and Independent States, they have full Power to levy War, conclude Peace, contract Alliances, establish Commerce, and to do all other Acts and Things which Independent States may of right do. And for the support of this Declaration, with a firm reliance on the protection of Divine Providence, we mutually pledge to each other our Lives, our Fortunes, and our sacred Honor.[141]

Beneath these words, at the bottom of the Declaration of Independence, each nation-state was itemized, along with the signers from that particular colony. Note that the states were listed, not as a single nationalized people, as the "United States of America," but separately, as individual political bodies, as, in fact, "States United of America"—each an autonomous country unto itself. Here is the actual text showing the names of the signatories along with their home countries (states):

New Hampshire: Josiah Bartlett, William Whipple, Matthew Thornton

Massachusetts: John Hancock, Samuel Adams, John Adams, Robert Treat Paine, Elbridge Gerry
Rhode Island: Stephen Hopkins, William Ellery
Connecticut: Roger Sherman, Samuel Huntington, William Williams, Oliver Wolcott
New York: William Floyd, Philip Livingston, Francis Lewis, Lewis Morris
New Jersey: Richard Stockton, John Witherspoon, Francis Hopkinson, John Hart, Abraham Clark
Pennsylvania: Robert Morris, Benjamin Rush, Benjamin Franklin, John Morton, George Clymer, James Smith, George Taylor, James Wilson, George Ross
Delaware: Caesar Rodney, George Read, Thomas McKean
Maryland: Samuel Chase, William Paca, Thomas Stone, Charles Carroll of Carrollton
Virginia: George Wythe, Richard Henry Lee, Thomas Jefferson, Benjamin Harrison, Thomas Nelson, Jr., Francis Lightfoot Lee, Carter Braxton
North Carolina: William Hooper, Joseph Hewes, John Penn
South Carolina: Edward Rutledge, Thomas Heyward, Jr., Thomas Lynch, Jr., Arthur Middleton
Georgia: Button Gwinnett, Lyman Hall, George Walton[142]

Further evidence comes from the May 16, 1778, Valley Forge Oath of future U.S. President James Monroe, who "acknowledged the United States of America to be free, independent, and sovereign states," whose people "thereof owe no allegiance or obedience" to anyone but their own state.[143]

Elbridge Gerry.

FACT 53

THE U.S. IS STILL A CONFEDERACY

From such documents the conclusion is clear: the United States of America began as a voluntary confederation of 13 individual nations with a weak central government, a confederated Union that was subordinate to those states.

After the Constitutional Convention of 1787 at Philadelphia, the Articles of Confederation were replaced by the U.S. Constitution. But our government remained a confederate republic, and each of the states retained all of the rights originally accorded to them as individual nation-states by the Declaration of Independence, the Articles of Confederation, the U.S. Constitution, and finally the Bill of Rights.

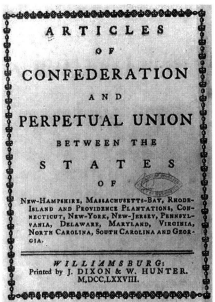

Title page of the Articles of Confederation, from 1778, listing the colonies as States United not "United States."

FACT 54

LINCOLN'S ELECTION LAUNCHED THE BIRTH OF THE SOUTHERN CONFEDERACY

In one of the more bizarre incidents in American history, after ascending to the White House, Abraham Lincoln chose to dismiss these bold facts, as if none of them were true or indeed had ever even existed. Like big government Liberals today, he detested the Founding Fathers' individualistic concept of confederation, with its accompanying entitlements of states' rights and secession.

It is little wonder then that the Southern Confederacy got its start on November 6, 1860, the day white supremacist Lincoln (a Republican, the Liberal Party at the time) was elected America's sixteenth president on a platform promising *not* to interfere with slavery (as he clearly states in his Inaugural Address on March 4, 1861, and as was asserted obliquely in the 1860 Republican Party Platform).[144]

The State Sovereignty Flag of South Carolina.

FACT 55

SOUTHERN CONSERVATIVES & THE ELECTORAL COLLEGE INADVERTENTLY HELPED INSTITUTE THE CONFEDERATE STATES OF AMERICA

Had the Conservatives (at that time the Democrats) stood together and not divided their vote, Lincoln would have gone down in abject defeat. Instead, he won, in great part, because not only did ten of the Southern states refuse to put him on their ballots, but also because the majority of Northerners at the time were anti-abolition. For his was the only party that pledged to allow slavery to continue unimpeded (though, due to entrenched Yankee racism, it was against the expansion of slavery outside the South).[145]

This made Lincoln the first sectionally elected president in U.S. history, and that with only 39 percent of the popular American vote. Thus the Southern Confederacy was born, in part, due to our, by then, already outdated Electoral College.[146]

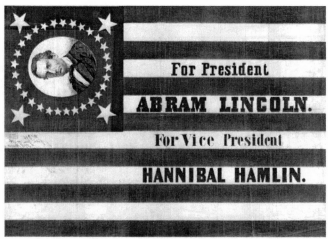

1860 campaign banner of the Republican Party (then the Liberal Party).

FACT 56

THE SECOND OR SOUTHERN C.S.A. WAS A LEGALLY FORMED REPUBLIC OF 13 SOVEREIGN NATION-STATES

Howell Cobb.

T hough the first Southern state to secede from the Union after Lincoln's election was South Carolina (on December 20, 1860), it was not until February 4, 1861, that the Southern Confederacy was officially founded under the political leadership of Howell Cobb, president of the Provisional Confederate Congress. Constitutionally "organized as a separate and independent republic," the C.S.A. was a legally formed foreign country within the boundaries of North America, now completely disassociated from the United States of America.[147] This makes the phrase "Civil War," defined as "a conflict between states belonging to the same nation," one of the great misnomers of American history![148]

Six Southern states had seceded from the Union by then: South Carolina, Mississippi, Florida, Alabama, Georgia, and Louisiana. What follows are the opening words of the First Session of the Provisional Confederate Congress at the (first) Confederate Capitol in Montgomery, Alabama, on February 4, 1861.[149] Also included here is South Carolina's ordinance of secession—as an example of the general tone of the secession ordinances of the other Southern states:

> Be it remembered that on the fourth day of February, in the year of our Lord one thousand eight hundred and sixty-one, and in the Capitol of the State of Alabama, in the city of Montgomery, at the hour of noon, there assembled certain deputies and delegates from the several independent Southern States of North America, to wit:

Alabama, Florida, Georgia, Louisiana, Mississippi, and South Carolina; the said delegates and deputies being thus assembled and convened under and by virtue of divers ordinances and resolutions adopted by the several conventions of the peoples of the independent States aforenamed; which said ordinances and resolutions are severally as follows:

An ordinance to dissolve the Union between the State of South Carolina and the other States united with her under the compact entitled 'The Constitution of the United States of America.' We the people of the State of South Carolina, in convention assembled do declare and ordain and it is hereby declared and ordained, that the ordinance adopted by us in convention, on the 23rd day of May, in the year of our Lord 1788, whereby the Constitution of the United States of America was ratified, and also all acts and parts of acts of the general assembly of this State, ratifying amendments of the said Constitution, are hereby repealed, and that the Union now subsisting between South Carolina and other States under the name of the United States of America is hereby dissolved. Unanimously adopted 20th day of December, A.D. 1860.[150]

By November 1861 a total of 11 Southern states and portions of two Southern states had seceded. According to official records the order of Southern state secession was as follows:[151]

1. SOUTH CAROLINA: December 20, 1860.[152]
2. MISSISSIPPI: January 9, 1861.[153]
3. FLORIDA: January 10, 1861.[154]
4. ALABAMA: January 11, 1861.[155]
5. GEORGIA: January 19, 1861.[156]
6. LOUISIANA: January 26, 1861.[157]
7. TEXAS: February 1, 1861 (not formally ratified until February 23).[158]
8. VIRGINIA: April 17, 1861.[159]
9. ARKANSAS: May 6, 1861.[160]
10. NORTH CAROLINA: May 20, 1861.[161]
11. TENNESSEE: June 8, 1861.[162]
12. MISSOURI: October 31, 1861 (only a portion of the state seceded).[163]
13. KENTUCKY: November 20, 1861 (only a portion of the state seceded).[164]

FACT 57

THE SOUTHERN CONFEDERACY WAS NAMED AFTER ONE OF THE EARLY NAMES FOR THE UNITED STATES: "CONFEDERATE STATES OF AMERICA"

The Southern Confederacy possessed 13 seceded states in all, which were symbolized by a 13 star circle on its First National Flag. This, of course, was the same number of colonial states that had seceded from England to form the first Confederate States of America in 1781, and which were astrally symbolized on the U.S. Confederate flag of that period, and which is still known as the "Betsy Ross Flag."

The first official flag of the U.S., the "Betsy Ross" had a 13 star circle representing the colonies of Delaware, Pennsylvania, New Jersey, Georgia, Connecticut, Massachusetts, Maryland, South Carolina, New Hampshire, Virginia, New York, North Carolina, and Rhode Island.

Furthermore, despite a few significant alterations, the Southern Confederacy very precisely patterned its Constitution on the Constitution of the United States, a document that was, in turn, built around our country's first Constitution, the Articles of Confederation, formulated during the period of American Confederation (1781-1789).

Lastly, like the U.S.A., the C.S.A. was intentionally formed to be a "lasting confederacy": a perpetual union of powerful autonomous states existing under a small limited central government.

It is obvious then why the Southern Confederate Founding Fathers gave their new republic the name "the Confederate States of America." As we have seen, this was the name given to the original U.S.A. by both American citizens and foreigners, and more loosely by the American Founding Fathers and countless subsequent statesmen and politicians, from George Washington and Thomas Jefferson to Jefferson Davis and Abraham Lincoln.

From these few facts alone it is patently clear why the C.S.A. chose its name: *the second Confederate States of America (1861) was meant to be a continuation of the first or original Confederate States of America (1781)*, not a rebellion intent on "destroying the United States," as anti-South critics continue to misleadingly assert.

The "Betsy Ross" 13 star flag of the U.S. Confederacy, 1781.

The "First National" 13 star flag of the Southern Confederacy, 1861.

FACT 58

THE C.S.A. BANNED THE FOREIGN SLAVE TRADE NINE MONTHS BEFORE THE U.S.A.

On March 11, 1861, the Southern Confederacy issued its new constitution. Here the Southern Confederate Founders borrowed, as mentioned, not only the wording of the Constitution of the United States of America (U.S.A.), they also copied the U.S. Confederate Founders of 1781 by giving theirs the name "The Constitution of the Confederate States of America" (C.S.A.).

This important American document included a clause prohibiting all foreign slave trading within its borders.[165] This was nine months before the Thirteenth Amendment finally banned slavery across the U.S.[166]

Meeting of the Southern Confederate Congress, 1861, Howell Cobb presiding.

FACT 59

LINCOLN INTENTIONALLY DRAGGED
THE SOUTHERN CONFEDERACY INTO WAR

On April 12, 1861, in order to force his left-wing agenda on the conservative South, Lincoln nefariously tricked the Confederacy into firing the first shot at the Battle of Fort Sumter.

Though no one was killed (the South only wanted all U.S. troops removed from the island—which now belonged to the C.S.A.), Lincoln mendaciously accused the South of aggressing on the U.S. flag, and on April 15 called for 75,000 Federal troops to invade Dixie.

The Southern Confederacy had no choice but to defend its territory and people against Lincoln and his illicit and aggressive interlopers. Thus was born the conflict incorrectly known in the North as the "Civil War."[167]

The Battle of Fort Sumter, April 12-14, 1861.

FACT 60

CONFEDERATE PRESIDENT JEFFERSON DAVIS SAID THAT THE WAR WAS NOT OVER SLAVERY

Clearly slavery had nothing to do with the Southern Confederacy and Lincoln's War. How do we know? Because the political and military leaders of both the Confederacy and the Union said so.

Here is how C.S. President Jefferson Davis put it:

> The truth remains intact and incontrovertible, that the existence of African servitude was in no wise the cause of the conflict, but only an incident. In the later controversies that arose, however, its effect in operating as a lever upon the passions, prejudices, or sympathies of mankind, was so potent that it has been spread like a thick cloud over the whole horizon of historic truth.[168]

Jefferson Davis.

FACT 61

CONFEDERATE VICE PRESIDENT ALEXANDER H. STEPHENS SAID THAT THE WAR WAS NOT OVER SLAVERY

To the last day of his life our celebrated vice president, Alexander H. Stephens, declared that the South seceded for one reason and one reason only: to "render our liberties and institutions more secure" by "rescuing, restoring, and re-establishing the Constitution."

As for the War, the South took up arms, he often noted, for no other reason than a "desire to preserve constitutional liberty and perpetuate the government in its purity."[169]

Alexander H. Stephens.

FACT 62

CONFEDERATE GENERAL ROBERT E. LEE SAID THAT THE WAR WAS NOT OVER SLAVERY

Accordding to Robert E. Lee, the South's highest ranking military officer:

> All the South has ever desired was that the Union as established by our forefathers should be preserved; and that the government as originally organized should be administered in purity and truth.[170]

Robert E. Lee.

FACT 63

UNION PRESIDENT ABRAHAM LINCOLN SAID THAT THE WAR WAS NOT OVER SLAVERY

Here is what U.S. President Abraham Lincoln said about the true Cause of the War—and it was not about slavery:

> My enemies pretend I am now carrying on this war for the sole purpose of abolition. So long as I am President, it shall be carried on for the sole purpose of restoring the Union. . . . If there be those who would not save the Union unless they could at the same time destroy slavery, I do not agree with them. My paramount object in this struggle is to save the Union, and is not either to save or to destroy slavery. If I could save the Union without freeing any slave I would do it . . .[171]

Mainstream historians and the Liberal media like to gloss over these words, so we must repeat them here to preserve the truth for posterity: if "Honest Abe" were alive today, he would consider those who claim that the "Civil War" was fought over slavery his "enemies"!

Abraham Lincoln.

FACT 64

THE U.S. CONGRESS SAID THAT THE WAR WAS NOT OVER SLAVERY

The U.S. Congress also asserted that the Civil War had no connection to slavery. On July 22, 1861, it issued the following resolution:

> . . . this war is not waged upon our part in any spirit of oppression, nor for any purpose of conquest or subjugation, *nor purpose of overthrowing or interfering with the rights or established institutions [that is, slavery] of those States*; but to defend and maintain the supremacy of the Constitution and to preserve the Union with all the dignity, equality, and rights of the several States unimpaired; that as soon as these objects are accomplished the war ought to cease.[172]

U.S. Congress.

FACT 65

UNION GENERAL ULYSSES S. GRANT SAID THAT THE WAR WAS NOT OVER SLAVERY

The North's top military officer, Ulysses S. Grant, made this comment on the topic of slavery and the Cause of the War:

> The sole object of this war is to restore the union. Should I be convinced it has any other object, or that the government designs using its soldiers to execute the wishes of the Abolitionists, I pledge to you my honor as a man and a soldier, I would resign my commission and carry my sword to the other side.[173]

Ulysses S. Grant.

FACT 66

LINCOLN FOUGHT THE SOUTHERN CONFEDERACY IN ORDER TO INSTALL BIG GOVERNMENT AT WASHINGTON

Why was the War fought then, if not over slavery? Lincoln claimed it was to "preserve the union." But this was just a smokescreen to conceal his true Liberal agenda: to install big government, then known as the "American System," in Washington.[174]

Devised and promoted by Lincoln's political hero, slave owner Henry Clay[175]—a man "Dishonest Abe" called "my *beau ideal* of a statesman, the man for whom I fought all my humble life"[176]—the American System was a nationalist program in which there was to be a single sovereign authority, the president, who was to assume the role of a kinglike ruler with autocratic powers.

Likewise, the government at Washington, D.C. was to be federated, acting as a consolidated superpower that would eventually control the money supply, offer internal improvements,[177] intervene in foreign affairs, nationalize the banking system,[178] issue soaring tariffs, grant subsidies to corporations, engage in protectionism, and impose an income tax,[179] all hints of Lincoln's coming empire.[180]

In essence, what the American System proposed was a federated government that was the polar opposite of a confederated government. Under federation, its proponents, the Federalists, Monarchists, or Hamiltonians (named after Liberal Alexander Hamilton), as they were variously called,[181] not only sought to create a large, domineering, all-powerful, nationalized government to which all interests (from private to business) were subordinate,[182] but they also proposed that the states be largely stripped of their independence and authority, then placed in an inferior role. Hamilton himself wanted to get rid of the states completely.[183] Jeffersonianism was to be abolished and replaced with the Hamiltonian or American system.

As such, nation-building nationalist Lincoln must be considered nothing less than the "Great Federator": the creator of American big government for big business, with its big spending, Big Brother mind-set.[184] He is also either fully or partially responsible for the following: America's internal revenue program (the IRS), American protectionism, American imperialism, American expansionism, America's bloated military despotism, America's enormous standing army, America's central banking system, America's corporate welfare system (which Lincoln called "internal improvements"), America's nation-building

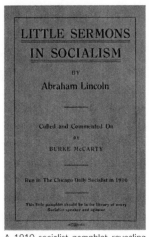

LITTLE SERMONS
IN SOCIALISM
BY
Abraham Lincoln
——
Culled and Commented On
BY
BURKE McCARTY
——
Ran in The Chicago Daily Socialist in 1910
——
This little pamphlet should be in the library of every
Socialist speaker and agitator
——

A 1910 socialist pamphlet revealing the real Abraham Lincoln.

agenda, and America's deeply entangled foreign alliances. (Lincoln apparently never read Jefferson's admonition that America's approach to foreign affairs should be: "Peace, commerce, and honest friendship with all nations, entangling alliances with none.")[185]

Is it any wonder that anti-Confederacy Lincoln surrounded himself with Marxists,[186] that he was supported by a group of radical socialists called the "Forty-Eighters,"[187] or that he has been adored by nationalists, dictators, and communists from around the world,[188] including socialists like Adolf Hitler[189] and Francis Bellamy (author of America's *Pledge of Allegiance*)?[190] And here, politically at least, is Lincoln's greatest legacy, for big government opened the door to federal tyranny and its many dangers and horrors: the consolidation of governmental powers, the centralization of Executive power, unchecked presidential power, the growth of the nanny state, unlimited abuses and corruption, and the progressive, intrusive, oppressive, tax-and-spend government that American citizens now labor under, whether they are Lincolnian Liberals themselves, or Independent, Conservative, or Libertarian. And all at the expense of individual civil liberties and states' rights.[191]

FACT 67

LINCOLN'S LIBERAL IDEAS ABOUT GOVERNMENT COUNTERED THOSE ESTABLISHED BY THE U.S. CONFEDERACY & THE FOUNDING FATHERS

Naturally everything about Clay's and Lincoln's American System was repugnant to traditional Southerners, a group that referred to itself as the Antifederalists or Jeffersonians (after Conservative Thomas Jefferson).[192] South Carolina statesman John C. Calhoun prophetically referred to the American System as "a dangerous and growing disease,"[193] one that would someday bring about the ruin of our delicately balanced confederate republic.[194]

Why was the American System anathema to the Jeffersonians? Because it went counter to the ideas set forth by the Founders in their formation of the American Confederacy, the system of government favored by Southerners; Conservative men like North Carolinian Thomas Burke, a member of the Continental Congress who, in 1777, first proposed an amendment to the Articles of Confederation which would severely curtail the powers of the central government while allowing the states to maintain their independence and sovereignty.[195] (Burke's recommendation became Article Two in the Articles of Confederation, the Tenth Amendment in the U.S. Constitution, and Article Six, Clause Six in the C.S. Constitution.)

Another Southerner, President Thomas Jefferson, a man who put his faith in ordinary people rather than in institutions,[196] had intended for America to be built on the farmer, its economy on agriculture, and its government on republicanism (then nearly akin to what we now call libertarianism). He distrusted the world of manufacturing, banking and foreign trade, believing that it led to class divisions, economic chaos, and mob rule.[197] Instead, he preferred an agrarian economy built around a simple equalitarian republic, even if it meant slowing the growth of the national economy.[198]

The Liberal Hamiltonians, on the other hand, wanted to replace the farmer with the merchant, agrarianism with industrialism, republicanism with a type of socialism.[199] Their emphasis was on making money, even if it meant economic inequality in American society.[200] They also wanted to dilute sectional differences between North and South and establish a strong permanent national army, both hostile ideas in the traditional South.[201]

Tragically, the Founders' agriculturally-based Confederacy, with its small, weak central government, would soon be overturned by Lincoln's industrially-based, federated American System, with its massive, all-powerful central government. As we have seen, the liberalizing process toward empire was already well underway long before Lincoln. It was Lincoln, however, who attempted to finish the job using total war on the American people and the Constitution.

Henry Clay.

FACT 68

DAVIS DECLARED THAT THE CONFEDERACY FOUGHT FOR THE "INHERENT RIGHT" OF INDIVIDUAL STATE SOVEREIGNTY

The always perspicacious Jefferson Davis summarized Lincoln's "Civil War" this way:

> . . . the war was, on the part of the United States Government, one of aggression and usurpation, and, on the part of the South, was for the defense of an inherent, unalienable right.[202]

What was that right? The right of state sovereignty and self-determination as laid out in the Declaration of Independence, the Articles of Confederation, the Bill of Rights, and the Constitution itself (see the Ninth and Tenth Amendments in particular).[203]

Jefferson Davis.

FACT 69

THE AMERICAN CIVIL WAR WAS A CONSERVATIVE VS. LIBERAL CONFLICT

The "Civil War" then did not concern slavery. Rather as Confederate Vice President Alexander H. Stephens and others repeatedly noted, it was a battle between what they then called "Consolidationists" or "Centralists" (that is, Liberals who wanted to consolidate all power in the federal government) and "Federalists" or "Constitutionalists" (that is, Conservatives who wanted to maintain states' rights and the constitutional separation of powers.[204]

In essence the Civil War was a battle between Southern agrarianism and Northern industrialism;[205] between the farming and commerce capitalism of the South and the finance and industry capitalism of the North;[206] between Southern free trade and Northern protective tariffs;[207] between Southern traditionalism and Northern progressivism; between Southern ruralism (the countryman) and Northern urbanism (the townsman); between Southern conservatism and Northern liberalism; between the South's desire to maintain Thomas Jefferson's "Confederate Republic" and the North's desire to change it into Alexander Hamilton's federate democracy.[208]

Shorn of Northern myth and anti-South propaganda, Lincoln's War was nothing but a conflict that pitted liberal, progressive, Northern industrialists who cared little for the Constitution, against conservative, traditional, Southern agriculturalists who were strict constitutionalists.[209]

As we are all well aware, this Liberal vs. Conservative conflict still rages on today, just as potently as it did in the 1860s.[210]

FACT 70

THERE HAVE BEEN TWO
"CONFEDERATE STATES OF AMERICA"

P ro-North historians like to pretend that the name the South chose for its new republic, "the Confederate States of America," was invented on the spot as a further act of "rebellion" against the Union. Nothing could be further from the truth.

As we have seen, the Southern Founding Fathers intentionally borrowed it from the name the U.S. Founding Fathers originally gave to the United States of America: "the Confederacy," which for all practical purposes meant "the Confederate States of America."

And this is exactly what Rhode Island minister David S. Rowland called the U.S. in 1779,[211] it is what an anonymous English author called it in 1782,[212] and it is what Tocqueville called America in 1832.[213]

This is also why James Madison referred to the U.S. as "the present Confederation of the American States."[214] And it is why Thomas Jefferson called the U.S. a "lasting Confederacy,"[215] and it is why, even after the Articles of Confederation were replaced by the U.S. Constitution, George Washington referred to the U.S. as "the new Confederacy."[216]

In 1861 Southerners gave their own new republic this same name, "the Confederate States of America," and for the same reason: the desire to reap the many benefits of living in a confederate republic, a country made up of powerful, self-governing, independent states operating under a small, limited central government.

FACT 71

THE SOUTHERN CONFEDERACY LOST THE WAR BECAUSE OF LINCOLN'S IMMORALITY

There were many factors that led up to the South's loss, of course, and which contributed to Lee's so-called "surrender" on April 9, 1865. But there are two reasons that are often overlooked and seldom discussed: Abraham Lincoln's criminal mind and Jefferson Davis' law-abiding mind.

Lincoln assured a Yankee victory by subverting the Constitution,[217] engaging in political chicanery (such as rigging elections[218] and posting armed guards at polling stations to intimidate voters)[219] and countless war crimes (such as arresting and torturing Northern peace advocates,[220] allowing the theft, abuse, rape and murder of Southern civilians),[221] disregarding the Geneva Convention (by sanctioning total war on the South),[222] and psychologically and emotionally manipulating the Northern populace.[223] Davis, on the other hand, helped guarantee Southern defeat by honoring the Confederate Constitution, avoiding political skullduggery, holding his troops to a high standard of behavior, observing the Geneva Convention, discouraging subversive activity among his soldiers, and being honest with the Southern people.[224]

Tragically, Davis, his advisors, and his military officers all woefully underestimated the arrogance, aggressiveness, guile, inhumanity, greed, self-delusion, and violence of their chief foe, big government Liberal, megalomanic Lincoln, who, just as progressives do today, despised the idea of states' rights, and who put socialistic idealism[225] not only above the political intentions of the Constitution and the Founding Generation, but above commonsense and practicality as well.[226] The result? A bloated American Empire, now with hundreds of departments and millions of employees that control nearly facet of its citizens' lives.

FACT 72

THE SOUTHERN CONFEDERACY LIVES ON

D espite the birth and growth of the Lincolnian Empire, however, the Southern Confederacy, the second Confederate States of America, was never "destroyed," as Yankee myth teaches. It was never "closed down," never officially made "nonexistent." It is still a legitimate, existing, constitutionally created republic.

Lee "surrendering" to Grant.

It is true that Confederate General Robert E. Lee signed Grant's "surrender agreement" on April 9, 1865.[227] But even though he was the highest ranking Rebel military officer at the time, Lee lacked the authority to make such a momentous political decision. The Confederate Congress, the only body with such power,[228] never signed a single sheet of paper authorizing the termination of the Confederate government, the permanent suspension of the Confederate Constitution, or the dissolution of the Confederate States.

All are technically still intact and active, awaiting the right time and the right individuals to relaunch what St. George Tucker called the "Confederate Republic,"[229] Thomas Jefferson's "lasting Confederacy";[230] what Tocqueville and many others called "the Confederate States of America"[231]—*the government originally intended by the U.S. Founding Fathers.*[232]

FACT 73

THE SOUTHERN CONFEDERACY FOUGHT OFF AN ARMY SUPERIOR IN SIZE FOR FOUR YEARS

The second Confederate States of America, that is, the Southern Confederacy of 1861, was without doubt one of the most remarkable political bodies in the history of the world.

For instance, though the North possessed three times the manpower, money, and supplies, the Southern Confederacy was able to keep Lincoln's armies engaged on the battlefield for four long years. It was victorious in numerous battles big and small (often against much larger forces with better weapons), as well, and, according to U.S. General Ulysses S. Grant, the Confederacy would have won the entire War had it simply prolonged it for just one more year.[233]

Combined, these facts alone must be considered one of the greatest military achievements in the annals of mankind.[234]

The Battle of Balls Bluff, October 21, 1861, just one of many Confederate victories.

FACT 74

THE SOUTHERN CONFEDERACY CAREFULLY PROTECTED ITS BLACK SERVANTS

The Southern Confederacy is famous for scores of other little known facts as well. While there were almost no laws protecting black slaves in the Old North, in the Old South there were countless rules, regulations, and statutes that guarded the Confederacy's black servants from the rare cruel slaver, prevented the breakup of slave families, and which provided them with numerous human rights and freedoms that are not part of authentic slavery—such as that found both then and today in Africa.[235]

Well dressed, well fed, well cared for Southern "slaves."

FACT 75

THE SOUTHERN CONFEDERACY WAS FAR LESS RACIST THAN THE UNION

A ccording to foreign travelers and tourists to the U.S., there was far less racism in the Southern Confederacy than in the Union. Even many Yankee visitors to the C.S.A. made note of the general lack of racial bias throughout the Confederate population,[236] also commenting on the warm relationships between white masters and black servants.[237]

After touring the North and South in the early 1830s, Frenchman Alexis de Tocqueville wrote:

> Whosoever has inhabited the United States must have perceived that in those parts of the Union in which the negroes are no longer slaves, they have in nowise drawn nearer to the whites. On the contrary, the prejudice of the race appears to be stronger in the States which have abolished slavery than in those where it still exists; and nowhere is it so intolerant as in those States where servitude never has been known.[238]

Southern whites and blacks enjoying one another's companionship in Old Dixie.

FACT 76

TRUE SLAVERY WAS NEVER PRACTICED IN THE SOUTHERN CONFEDERACY

The pro-North movement has long enjoyed belittling the Confederacy for "practicing slavery." The fact is, however, that *authentic* slavery did not exist in the Old South.

An authentic slave is defined as someone who is completely owned by another human being (as a piece of personal property) for life, and who possesses no human rights whatsoever.

Authentic slavery (shown here), once found among the early Egyptians, Greeks, Romans, Chinese, and Native-Americans—and still practiced in places like Africa—is an unfathomably cruel, barbaric, and sadistic form of bondage that was completely unknown in the Southern Confederacy.

This type of bondage was unknown in the Confederacy, where so-called "slaves" lived under the protection of hundreds of civil codes and rights, and could purchase their freedom at any time.

In truth, the "slavery" practiced in the Confederacy was just what President Jefferson Davis and many others said it was: "a mild form of indentured servitude" that was similar to peasantry and in many cases even apprenticeship.

This is why, after all, Southerners called their black bondsmen and women "servants" rather than the inaccurate and misleading Northern term "slaves."²³⁹

FACT 77

THE CONFEDERATE STATES OF AMERICA WAS NOT A "SLAVE REGIME"

The Confederate States of America was not a "slave regime" or a "slavocracy," as anti-South partisans have maliciously and incorrectly named it. In 1860 only 4.8 percent of the total white male population of the South owned black servants, and this in the same region where the American abolition movement was born. This is hardly what could be called a "slave regime"![240]

America did indeed have its slave regimes, but they were not in the South.

The first slavocracies existed among Native-Americans, who enslaved one another as a routine aspect of Indian society, using some of the most brutal and sadistic forms of slavery ever recorded. After European colonization, Native-Americans began enslaving untold thousands of whites, blacks, and browns as well.

New York state, North America's one and only great slave regime, engaged in the slave trade for 239 years, far longer than any other state North or South.

America's greatest slavocracy, however, emerged among the white colonists of the Northeast, where both the American slave trade and American slavery were born in the early 1600s. Of these states, New York came to be "America's Slave Capital," a true slave regime that imported and sold millions of (previously enslaved) Africans over a period of 239 years, far longer than any other state, North or South.[241]

FACT 78

THE SOUTHERN CONFEDERACY NEVER ENGAGED IN THE SLAVE TRADE

The only American slave ships to ever sail from the U.S. left from Northern ports aboard Northern slave vessels, that were designed by Northern engineers, constructed by Northern shipbuilders, fitted out by Northern riggers, piloted by Northern ship captains, manned by Northern crews, launched from Northern marine ports, funded by Northern businessmen, all which was supported by the vast majority of the anti-abolitionist Northern population.

In other words, the American slave trade was a purely Yankee business, one that operated under the auspices of, not the Confederate Flag, but the U.S. Flag.

The South did not own slave ships and never traded in foreign slaves. Her slavery was strictly domestic. This is one of the reasons she banned the foreign slave trade in the Confederacy's new Constitution, penned by the Confederate Founding Fathers in 1861.

American slavery got its start in the Northern states, which is why the American slave trade was an exclusively Yankee business.

Thus, while no slave ship ever flew under the Confederate Flag, it is this very flag that is today universally viewed as a "symbol of slavery." Such has been the overwhelming power of the North's revisionist version of American history that lies, slander, and disinformation concerning the Southern Confederacy have come to be regarded as fact![242] I call this "The Great Yankee Coverup," and have devoted an entire book to it.[243]

FACT 79

THE SOUTHERN CONFEDERACY PLANNED TO END SLAVERY BEFORE THE U.S. DID

In January 1865 Confederate Secretary of State Judah P. Benjamin ordered Confederate commissioner Duncan F. Kenner to England to announce the C.S.'s commitment to full emancipation. This was nearly a year before the U.S. issued the Thirteenth Amendment (on December 6) banning slavery throughout the nation.[244] (Let us note here that, contrary to Yankee mythology, the Northern states *never* officially abolished slavery. Instead they slowly and methodically destroyed the institution through a long drawn out process known as "gradual emancipation," taking over 100 years to complete the process, which finally ended in 1865 with the ratification of the Thirteenth Amendment. Tragically, the North refused to grant the South the same privilege, and instead demanded "immediate abolition," an impossibility at the time.)[245]

The Confederacy's motion to abolish slavery across the South had the complete support of the Southern populace, of course, the very people who had inaugurated the American abolition movement in the early 1700s.[246] One of the better known of the great Southern abolitionists was the celebrated antislavery Virginian, Robert E. Lee, who, on December 27, 1856—five years before Lincoln's War—made this comment about the "peculiar institution":

> There are few, I believe, in this enlightened age, but what will acknowledge that slavery as an institution is a moral and political evil in any country. It is idle to expatiate on its disadvantages. I think it is a greater evil to the white than to the colored race.[247]

Later, during the War, like *all* Southern civilians and Confederate soldiers and officers, Lee supported the idea of immediate abolition and black enlistment, a fact you will never read in any mainstream, pro-North "history" of the Civil War.[248]

FACT 80

FIFTY PERCENT OF THE CONFEDERATE ARMY WAS COMPRISED OF AFRICAN-AMERICANS

Though our mainstream history books tell us that Southern blacks did not support the Confederacy, the opposite is true. From surviving records we know that unofficially some 300,000 blacks donned Confederate gray, and went off to fight "Massa Linkum's" soldiers.

Hundreds of thousands of Southern blacks proudly and courageously fought for the 1861 Confederacy. This man, Private Louis Napoleon Nelson (the Confederacy's only known black chaplain), served under General Nathan Bedford Forrest, fought at numerous battles, and attended scores of Confederate reunions after the War ended. Louis' grandson, Nelson W. Winbush, wrote the foreword for one of the author's books.

And these numbers are conservative if we use the definition of a "private soldier" as determined by German-American Union general, August Valentine Kautz, in 1864: "Any man in the military service who receives pay, whether sworn in or not, is a soldier, because he is subject to military law."[249]

Using Kautz's definition of a "private soldier," some 2 million Southerners fought in the Confederacy: 1 million whites and perhaps as many as 1 million blacks. As most of the 4 million blacks (3.5 million servants, 500,000 free) living in the South at the time of Lincoln's War remained loyal to Confederacy, and as at least 500,000 to 1 million of these either worked in or fought in the Rebel army and navy in some capacity, Kautz' definition raises the percentage of Southern blacks who defended the Confederacy as real soldiers to as much as 50 percent of the total Confederate soldier population, five times the number that fought for the Union![250]

FACT 81

THE CONFEDERATE MILITARY WAS MULTIRACIAL, MULTICULTURAL, & MULTIETHNIC

We have been taught that the Confederate armies were "100 percent white," this due to the "boundless white racism" that existed across the Old South. We have already seen that the South was far less racist than the North, so it is obvious that this charge cannot be true. The South's army and navy, in fact, reflected the region's citizenship, which was made up of every race, creed, and nationality.

Though—thanks to the vicious Yankee custom of burning down Southern courthouses[251]—exact statistics are impossible to come by, Southern historians have determined that the

The Southern Confederate army was made up of all races, colors, and nationalities.

following numbers are roughly accurate. In descending numerical order the Confederate army and navy was composed of about 1 million European-Americans,[252] 300,000 to 1 million African-Americans,[253] 70,000 Native-Americans, 60,000 Latin-Americans,[254] 50,000 foreigners,[255] 12,000 Jewish-Americans,[256] and 10,000 Asian-Americans.[257]

True Southerners, of all races, continue to be proud of our region's multiracial history, and of the many contributions made to Dixie by individuals of all colors, creeds, and nationalities.[258]

FACT 82

THE CONFEDERATE STATES OF AMERICA HAD THE SUPPORT OF EUROPE

Mainstream history books would have us believe that the Southern Confederacy was all alone in her quest to be free of Liberal Northern imperialism. But again, this is false. The real reason Europe hesitated to give the South diplomatic recognition was because it feared offending and possibly provoking the U.S. into war, a frightening scenario that at one point almost became a reality.

William H. Seward.

Through Lincoln's secretary of state, William H. Seward, Lincoln privately threatened war on any nation that interfered with his invasion of the South,[259] in particular England and France,[260] where European sympathy for the Confederacy was the strongest.[261]

Lincoln's fears were warranted: England's and France's ruling classes were always highly interested in and supportive of the Confederate Cause,[262] while the English population as a whole expressed "widespread sentiment" in favor of recognizing the Confederacy as a sovereign nation.[263]

It was Lincoln's menacing warning, in place throughout the duration of the conflict, that prevented "neutral" Europe from publicly supporting "belligerent" Dixie, and which in turn prolonged the War, caused thousands of unnecessary deaths, and aided in the South's eventual downfall.[264]

FACT 83

THE CONFEDERATE BATTLE FLAG IS A SYMBOL OF THE MULTIRACIAL, CONSERVATIVE CHRISTIAN SOUTH

The Confederate Battle Flag (a distinctive military flag designed for specific use on the battlefield), with its striking blue cross, thirteen white stars, and bright red field, is now daily accused of being a symbol of white racism by the anti-South movement. But where did this meaning derive? Certainly not from the South itself. It comes from the fact that it is so often used by modern hate groups.

The reason such groups use this particular flag is the same reason pro-North groups charge the flag with white racism: a total lack of knowledge of *authentic* Southern history. For as has been made plain throughout this very book, the goals and dreams of the Confederacy were never about race, nor were they based on racism, or even slavery. The "Southern Cause," as it is called, was always about upholding the original Constitution of the Founding Fathers and this document's sacred Jeffersonian promise of states' rights, a small decentralized federal government, self-determination, and personal freedom.

The Confederate Battle Flag then turns out to be anything but a symbol of white racism or white supremacy. Those who created it never intended it to have this meaning, and those who fought under it never thought of it as having this meaning. If anything it would be more accurate to call our flag a symbol of racial inclusiveness and multiculturalism, one founded on the Christian principles extolled by Jesus, whose main tenants were love and universal brotherhood.[265]

The Confederate Battle Flag itself was designed around the Christian crosses of Great Britain's flag (Saint George's Cross), Scotland's flag (Saint Andrew's Cross), and Ireland's flag (Saint Patrick's Cross).[266]

FACT 84

THE SOUTHERN CONFEDERACY
WAS NEVER "RECONSTRUCTED"

So-called "Reconstruction" was a Liberal Yankee plan to overhaul and forcefully "Northernize" the South after its "defeat" in April 1865. As Lincoln brazenly said to Interior Department official T. J. Barnett: "The entire South needs to be obliterated and replaced with new businessmen and new ideas."[267]

Southerners responded to the violent insanity of carpetbag-scallywag rule just as they did to the North's first illegal invasion of their homeland in 1861: they "rebelled" a second time, and with the help of a new and more enlightened president, Rutherford B. Hayes, by 1877 they were able to drive the last hated Yankee soldiers out of the South that year.

Free at last from the iron fist of Yankee dictatorship, Southern families returned to their homes and reopened their shops and schools (what was left of them). Former Confederate officers were quickly voted into office and the Confederate Flag was proudly flown once again outside every house, farm, and storefront. With Dixie now in tatters, Southerners did their level best to pick up where they had left off before Lincoln's illegal invasion 16 years earlier.

In the end, like the "Civil War" itself, Reconstruction was an utter failure, doomed by the impossibility of its very mission: to make the leisurely, religious, agricultural South into an exact duplicate of the fast-paced, atheistic, industrialized North. Victorian traditional Southerners were not about to let this happen, and they succeeded!

Even many Yankees themselves realized the futility of trying to Northernize Dixie, correctly calling it "a fool's errand." One of these, Ohio carpetbagger Albion W. Tourgee, put it this way:

> The North and the South are simply convenient names for two
> distinct, hostile, and irreconcilable ideas,—two civilizations they
> are sometimes called, especially at the South. At the North there
> is somewhat more of intellectual arrogance; and we are apt to
> speak of the one as civilization, and of the other as a species of
> barbarism. These two must always be in conflict until the one
> prevails, and the other falls. To uproot the one, and plant the other
> in its stead, is not the work of a moment or a day. That was our
> mistake. We [Yankees] tried to superimpose the civilization, the
> idea of the North, upon the South at a moment's warning. We
> presumed, that, by the suppression of rebellion, the Southern white
> man had become identical with the Caucasian of the North in
> thought and sentiment; and that the slave, by emancipation, had
> become a saint and a Solomon at once. So we tried to build up
> communities there which should be identical in thought, sentiment,
> growth, and development, with those of the North. It was a fool's
> errand.[268]

Unfortunately, Lincoln's left wing liberal dream (to Northernize the
South) is still very much alive. Now aided by thousands of disloyal "New
South" scallywags, the sinister process to eliminate all Southernness from
Dixie continues, stronger now than ever before. At every opportunity
true Southerners continue to resist the anti-South movement's goal to
exterminate Southern society by harassing us, interfering with our rights,
outlawing our symbols, ignoring and censoring our books, banning our
flags, removing our statues, defacing our monuments, and ridiculing our
heroes, history, and heritage. To those who are committed to
Northernizing us, we say: heed the words of Mr. Tourgee![269]

For the Confederacy first created by the Colonial Founding Fathers in
1781 and reestablished by the Southern Confederate Founding Fathers
in 1861, lives on in the hearts and minds of millions of Southerners! It
is an immortal concept; an idea that cannot be killed, destroyed, or
suppressed. Why?

Because the Southern Cause is really the cause of freedom, the same
cause that the Greeks fought for against the Persians at the Battle of
Thermopylae some 2,500 year ago. Just as King Leonidas sought
freedom from Persian rule under King Xerxes I, the American Colonists
sought freedom from British rule under King George III—after

independence forming a confederacy of sovereign "little republics" or "nation-states," which Tocqueville accurately referred to as "the Confederate States of America."

Sir William Wallace was of the same mind. Though vastly outnumbered, on September 11, 1297, the bold Scottish knight and his small band of warriors crushed a massive English army at the Battle of Stirling Bridge. Scores of Scots died, yet theirs was considered a "beautiful death." Why? Because they had perished in an attempt to be free of the tyrannical rule of King Edward I.

In 1861 America's Southern people sought freedom from Yankee rule under "King Abraham," and in imitation of the U.S. Founding Generation, formed their own "Confederate States of America." It is this republican form of government, which Southern Conservative Thomas Jefferson called a "lasting Confederacy," that lives on in the souls of lovers of personal liberty everywhere.

Sir William Wallace.

APPENDIX

On the Confederacy

"In What Manner Republics Provide for Their Safety" by Baron de Montesquieu, from *The Spirit of Laws*, 1750

I f a republic is small, it is destroyed by a foreign force; if it be large, it is ruined by an internal imperfection. This twofold inconveniency is equally contagious to democracies and aristocracies, whether good or bad. The evil is in the very thing itself; and no form can redress it.

Very probable it is that mankind would have been at length obliged to live constantly under the government of a single person, had they not contrived a kind of constitution that has all the internal advantages of a republican, together with the external force of a monarchical, government. I mean a confederate republic.

This form of government is a convention by which several small states agree to become members of a larger one which they intend to form. It is a kind of assemblage of societies, that constitute a new one, capable of increasing by means of new associations, till they arrive to such a degree of power, as to be able to provide for the security of the whole united body.

It was these associations that contributed so long to the prosperity of Greece. By these the Romans attacked the universe, and by these only the universe withstood them: for when Rome was arrived to her highest pitch of grandeur, it was the associations behind the Danube and the Rhine, associations formed by the terror, that enabled the Barbarians to resist her power.

From hence it proceeds that Holland, Germany, and the Swiss Cantons, are considered in Europe as perpetual |confederate| republics.

The associations of cities were formerly more necessary than in our times. A weak defenceless town was exposed to greater dangers. By conquest it was deprived not only of the executive and legislative power, as at present, but moreover of all human property.

A |confederate| republic of this kind capable of withstanding an external force, may be able to support its greatness without any internal corruption; the form of this society prevents all manner of inconveniencies.

The member that would attempt to usurp over the rest, could not be supposed to have an equal authority and credit in all the confederate states. Were it to have too great an influence over one, this would alarm the rest; were it to subdue another, that which would still remain free, might withstand it with forces independent of those which the other had usurped, and overpower it before it could be settled in its usurpation.

Should a popular insurrection happen in one of the confederate states, the others are able to quell it. Should abuses creep into one part, they are reformed by those that remain found. The state may be destroyed on one side, and not on the other; the confederacy may be dissolved, and the confederates preserve their sovereignty.

As this government is composed of petty republics, it enjoys the internal happiness of each; and with respect to its external situation, it is possessed by means of the association, of all the advantages of large monarchies.

. . . The Canaanites were destroyed, by reason [that] they were petty monarchies that had no union nor confederacy for their common defence. This is because a confederacy is not agreeable to the nature of petty monarchies.

The confederate republic of Germany consists of free cities, and of petty states subject to different princes. Experience shews us that it is much more imperfect than that of Holland and Switzerland.

The spirit of monarchy is war and enlargement of dominion: peace and moderation is the spirit of a republic. These two kinds of government cannot naturally subsist in a confederate republic.

Thus we observe in the Roman history, that when the Veii [Veientes] had chosen a king, they were immediately abandoned by all the other petty republics of Tuscany. Greece was undone as soon as the kings of Macedon obtained a feat among the Amphictyons.

The confederate republic of Germany, composed of princes and free towns, subsists by means of a chief, who is in some measure the magistrate, and in some the monarch, of the union.

. . . In the [confederate] republic of Holland one province cannot conclude an alliance without the consent of the others. This law, which is an excellent one and even necessary in a confederate republic, is wanting in the Germanic constitution, where it would prevent the misfortunes that may happen to the whole confederacy, through the imprudence, ambition, or avarice of a single member. A republic united by a political confederacy, has given itself entirely up, and has nothing more to resign.

It is difficult for the united states to be all of an equal bigness and power. The Lycian republic was an association of twenty-three towns; the large ones had three votes in the common council, the middling ones two, and the small towns one. The Dutch republic consists of seven, great or small, provinces, that have each one voice.

The cities of Lycia contributed to the expences of the State, according to the proportion of suffrages. The provinces of the united Netherlands cannot follow this proportion; they must be directed by that of their power.

In Lycia the judges and town magistrates were elected by the common council, and according to the proportion already mentioned. In the [confederate] republic of Holland they are not chosen by the common council, but each town names its magistrates. Were I to give a model of an excellent confederate republic, I should pitch that of Lycia.[270]

NOTES

1. See e.g., Seabrook, TQJD, pp. 30, 38, 76.

2. Seabrook, EYWTATCWIW, p. 13.

3. The creation of our first Constitution, the Articles of Confederation, alone testifies to this fact: first proposed by North Carolinian Thomas Burke, Article Two, which stringently limits the powers of the central government while allowing the states to retain full sovereignty, was *overwhelming* supported by Congress in April 1777, leaving ultimate power to the individual states. This is the epitome of the concept of confederation. See Jensen, TNN, pp. 25-26.

4. Nivola and Rosenbloom, p. 70.

5. Brooks, p. 98.

6. For more on some of the early Native-American Confederacies, see Hodge, Vol. 1, pp. 2-4, 7, 8, 12, 21, 39-40, 42, 50-53, 68, 70, 83, 86, 89, 90, 102, 145, 162, 179, 181-182, 186-187, 202, 220, 238-241, 247, 249, 260, 263, 267, 272, 278, 286, 300, 321, 335, 337, 354, 363-364, 399, 405, 462, 475, 487, 507, 510, 524, 532, 535, 598-600, 638-639, 662, 682, 684, 705, 776, 781, 783, 786, 795-796, 800, 802, 810, 812, 817-818, 820-822, 826, 829, 840, 852, 856, 877-878, 909, 929-932, 934, 948-949, 962, 964.

7. Some early European-American writers viewed all Indian confederations as a single unit, which they referred to as "the confederacy of savages." Marshall, pp. 304-305.

8. Washington, Vol. 8, pp. 338, 340, 435, 437, 438, 440, 441.

9. Brooks, p. 100.

10. Beach, Vol. 3, s.v. "Calhoun, John Caldwell."

11. See Madison, Vols. 1, 2, and 3, pp. 35, 38, 39, 658, 780, 789, 874, 882, 889, 897, 951, 1004.

12. To this day Switzerland's official name is the "Swiss Confederation," or in Latin: *Confoederatio Helvetica*; in French: Confédération Suisse; in Italian: Confederazione Svizzera; and in Rumantsch: Confederaziun Svizzer.

13. Washington, Vol. 8, pp. 338, 340, 435, 437, 438, 440, 441.

14. Seabrook, TAOCE, p. 9.

15. Seabrook, TAOCE, p. 10.

16. Hamilton, Madison, and Jay, p. 21.

17. Collier and Collier, p. 4.

18. Encyc. Brit., s.v. "Federal Government."

19. Compton's Pic. Encyc., s.v. "States' Rights."

20. Seabrook, TAOCE, p. 10.

21. See Elliot, Vol. 2, pp. 138, 396, 399, 402, 403, 448, 449.

22. Elliot, Vol. 2, p. 261.

23. Bergh, Vol. 1, p. 47.

24. Bergh, Vol. 1, p. 48.

25. Seabrook, TAOCE, p. 15.

26. Washington, Vol. 5, p. 444.

27. Washington, Vol. 2, p. 301; Vol. 5, p. 164.

28. Washington, Vol. 8, pp. 447, 452.

29. Washington, Vol. 8, p. 414.

30. Seabrook, TAOCE, p. 16.

31. Debate continues as to whether these individuals were true U.S. presidents or merely heads of Congress. It is clear, in my opinion, however, that they were legitimate U.S. presidents, overseeing America's first Confederate States of America.

32. Seabrook, TAOCE, p. 41.

33. Confusingly, after 1787, these names changed meaning, with the conservative Federalists becoming "Anti-Federalists," and the liberal Nationalists becoming "Federalists."

34. Seabrook, TAOCE, p. 11.

35. Seabrook, TAOCE, p. 11.

36. Madison, Vol. 3, p. 1470.

37. Encyc. Brit., s.v. "Anti-Federalists"; "Federalist Party."

38. Seabrook, TAOCE, p. 6.

39. Bergh, Vol. 1, p. 48.

40. Napolitano, p. 118.

41. Ashe, pp. 21-22.

42. For more on the South's view of Lincoln, see Seabrook, AL, passim.

43. Banks, p. 186.

44. Hamilton, Madison, and Jay, p. 106.

45. Hamilton, Madison, and Jay, p. 89. See also M. D. Peterson, JM, pp. 102-103; Hacker, p. 213.

46. Hamilton, Madison, and Jay, p. 21.

47. Hamilton, Madison, and Jay, p. 65.

48. See e.g., S. M. Hamilton, Vol. 1, pp. 74, 83, 98, 102, 109, 110, 117, 118, 127, 130, 139, 140, 141, 142, 148, 150, 152, 157, 163, 195, 311, 312, 313, 314, 322, 324, 329, 338.

49. C. F. Adams, Vol. 8, p. 19.

50. Bergh, Vol. 15, p. 297.

51. M. D. Peterson, TJ, p. 1482.

52. Williams, Vol. 2, p. 1048.

53. Hacker, p. 420.

54. Ransom, p. 96.

55. Tyler, LTT, Vol. 3, pp. 67, 68.

56. Williams, Vol. 2, p. 1206.

57. DeGregorio, s.v. "James K. Polk" (p. 168).

58. During his presidency, Davis often worked out of the Confederate Capitol at Richmond, Virginia, designed by his namesake Thomas Jefferson. Channing, p. 168.

59. W. Davis, JD, p. 177.

60. Ransom, p. 99.

61. Litwack, NS, p. 49.

62. Nicolay and Hay, ALCW, Vol. 1, p. 143.

63. DeGregorio, s.v. "Franklin Pierce" (p. 203).

64. Nicolay and Hay, ALCW, Vol. 1, p. 487.

65. Nicolay and Hay, ALCW, Vol. 1, p. 138.

66. Nicolay and Hay, ALCW, Vol. 1, p. 606. Lincoln actually used the word Confederacy many dozens of times throughout his political career. See e.g., Nicolay and Hay, ALCW, Vol. 1, pp. 143, 168, 181, 345, 346, 487, 501, 611, 616, 624, 627, 628.

67. Nicolay and Hay, ALCW, Vol. 1, p. 691.

68. Findlay and Findlay, pp. 182-183.

69. Stephens, Vol. 1, pp. 157-158.

70. Elliot, Vol. 1, p. 137.

71. Elliot, Vol. 4, p. 537.

72. Register of Debates, Vol. 9, pp. 170, 171.

73. Williams, Vol. 2, Appendix, p. xxxvii. See also pp. 747, 887, 912, where Jackson calls the U.S.A. "our confederacy."

74. Hamilton, Madison, and Jay, p. 89. See also M. D. Peterson, JM, pp. 102-103; Hacker, p. 213.

75. See D. S. Rowland, passim.

76. A Man of No Party, p. 10.

77. Smith, passim.

78. Tocqueville, p. 169. Emphasis added.

79. Stephens, Vol. 1, p. 209.

80. Seabrook, TQJD, p. 34.

81. Stephens, Vol. 1, p. 236.

82. Seabrook, TAHSR, pp. 377-378.

83. Encyc. Brit., s.v. "Confederation."

84. Dilorenzo, RL, pp. 93-101.

85. Pollard, LC, p. 85.

86. Washington, Vol. 8, p. 420.

87. Marshall, p. 16.

88. J. Q. Adams, pp. 31, 37, 45.

89. C. Johnson, pp. 115-117.

90. For plotting with Alexander Hamilton against administration policy, Pickering was dismissed by Adams, the first and only secretary of state to be terminated in this manner. DeGregorio, s.v. "John Adams" (p. 28).

91. DeGregorio, s.v. "James Monroe" (p. 78).

92. C. King, Vol. 4, pp. 364-366.

93. Encyc. Brit., s.v. "Hartford"; C. Adams, p. 15.

94. DeGregorio, s.v. "James Madison" (p. 66).

95. Smelser, DR, p. 78.

96. Encyc. Brit., s.v. "Hartford."

97. Compton's Pic. Encyc., s.v. "States' Rights."

98. H. Adams, p. 351.

99. H. Adams, p. 338.

100. See Website: www.nps.gov/jela/the-treaty-of-ghent.htm.

101. During America's early history, in fact, Massachusetts threatened to secede from the Union on four different occasions, all without any violent resistance from any other state. Pollard, LC, p. 85.

102. DeGregorio, s.v. "Woodrow Wilson" (p. 411).

103. Pollard, LC, p. 96.

104. J. Davis, RFCG, Vol. 1, p. 54.

105. E. McPherson, PHUSAGR, pp. 49-50.

106. Buchanan was born in Pennsylvania.

107. On vacating the presidential chair for the last time, Buchanan told Lincoln: "My dear sir, if you are as happy on entering the White House as I on leaving it, you are a very happy man indeed." C. O'Brien, SLUSP, p. 83.

108. F. Moore, Vol. 7, p. 306.

109. Nicolay and Hay, ALCW, Vol. 2, p. 55.

110. Nicolay and Hay, ALCW, Vol. 2, p. 61.

111. See Seabrook, AL, pp. 106-110.

112. Findlay and Findlay, pp. 212-213.

113. Findlay and Findlay, pp. 214-217.

114. Hacker, p. 339.

115. Jensen, TNN, p. 347.

116. Tocqueville, p. 419.

117. Seabrook, TQJD, p. 40.

118. Rawle, p. 296.

119. Smelser, TDR, p. 78.

120. Upshur, p. 131. Emphasis added.

121. Randolph, p. 284.

122. J. Davis, RFCG, Vol. 1, p. 173.

123. J. Davis, RFCG, Vol. 2, p. 623.

124. J. Davis, RFCG, Vol. 1, p. 173.

125. Nicolay and Hay, ALCW, Vol. 2, p. 60.

126. Forman, p. 354.

127. Foley, p. 894.

128. Foley, p. 513.

129. Collier and Collier, p. 4.

130. Foley, pp. 212, 797.

131. Hamilton, Madison, and Jay, p. 21.

132. Washington, Vol. 8, p. 174.

133. Burns and Peltason, p. 41.

134. Ashe, pp. 17, 25.

135. Rouse, pp. 78-79.

136. Rosenbaum and Brinkley, s.v. "Antifederalists."

137. Dunbar Rowland, Vol. 1, p. 509.

138. See e.g., Foley, pp. 399, 900.

139. Garland, p. 103.

140. Henry, p. 16. The question of loyalty to state or nation was debated as early as 1787, at the Constitutional Convention in Philadelphia. Collier and Collier, p. 264. While most Northerners pledged their allegiance to the nation, well into the 1800s most Southerners chose to give their allegiance to their home states. This tradition lives on across Dixie to this day.

141. Rouse, p. 56.

142. Rouse, pp. 56-58.

143. S. M. Hamilton, Vol. 1, p. lxxv.

144. Seabrook, AL, pp. 55-56.

145. For more on 18th- and 19th-Century Yankee racism, see Seabrook, EYWTAASIW, passim.

146. Seabrook, EYWTAASIW, p. 51.

147. Journal of the Congress of the C.S.A., Vol. 1, p. 46.

148. See Seabrook, EYWTATCWIW, pp. 23-25.

149. For a host of reasons, in May 1861 President Jefferson Davis had the Confederate Capitol moved to Richmond, Virginia.

150. Journal of the Congress of the C.S.A., Vol. 1, p. 7.

151. The dates of secession can vary according to different sources and interpretations.

152. ORA, Ser. 4, Vol. 1, p. 1.

153. ORA, Ser. 4, Vol. 1, p. 42.

154. ORA, Ser. 4, Vol. 1, p. 54.

155. ORA, Ser. 4, Vol. 1, pp. 43-44.

156. ORA, Ser. 4, Vol. 1, p. 70.

157. ORA, Ser. 4, Vol. 1, p. 80.

158. Boatner, s.v. "Texas."

159. ORA, Ser. 4, Vol. 1, p. 223.

160. ORA, Ser. 4, Vol. 1, pp. 287-288.

161. ORA, Ser. 4, Vol. 1, pp. 335-336.

162. ORA, Ser. 4, Vol. 1, p. 290.

163. ORA, Ser. 4, Vol. 1, pp. 752-753.

164. ORA, Ser. 4, Vol. 1, p. 741.

165. Seabrook, EYWTAASIW, p. 51.

166. Seabrook, EYWTAASIW, p. 242.

167. For more on the truth about Lincoln and the Battle of Fort Sumter, see Seabrook, AL, pp. 105-133.

168. Seabrook, EYWTAASIW, p. 539.

169. Seabrook, TAHSR, p. 11.

170. Seabrook, EYWTAASIW, p. 1014.

171. Seabrook, AL, pp. 74, 378.

172. E. McPherson, PHUSAGR, p. 286. Emphasis added.

173. Meriwether, p. 219.

174. Rosenbaum and Brinkley, s.v. "American System"; DeGregorio, s.v. "John Quincy Adams"; Simpson, p. 75; Weintraub, pp. 48-49.

175. DeGregorio, s.v. "John Quincy Adams" (p. 97).

176. Nicolay and Hay, ALCW, Vol. 1, p. 299.

177. Like all Liberals, Lincoln liked the idea of the government bailing out mismanaged, bankrupt, and corrupt businesses, an idea then known as "internal improvements," but which we now more honestly refer to as "corporate welfare." See e.g., Lincoln's comment on, and support of, the internal improvement idea in Nicolay and Hay, ALCW, Vol. 1, p. 8.

178. Simpson, p. 75.

179. Rosenbaum and Brinkley, s.v. "American System."

180. Weintraub, pp. 48-49.

181. Today we would refer to the Federalists and Hamiltonians as Democrats; in other words, Liberals.

182. Woods, p. 34.

183. A. Cooke, ACA, p. 140.

184. For current news on the conservative fight against the big government that Lincoln helped install, see Website: www.breitbart.com.

185. Foley, p. 684; Weintraub, p. 44.

186. See Benson and Kennedy, passim.

187. Seabrook, HJDA, p. 68.

188. See DiLorenzo, LU, pp. 149-155.

189. Seabrook, EYWTATCWIW, pp. 120-121.

190. Seabrook, AL, pp. 506-507.

191. Napolitano, p. 76.

192. Today we would refer to the Antifederalists or Jeffersonians as Conservative Republicans, or in some cases Libertarians.

193. Crallé, Vol. 2, p. 224.

194. Coit, p. 249.

195. Jensen, TNN, p. 25.

196. Shorto, p. 124.

197. Hacker, pp. 247, 264.

198. Bernhard, p. 18.

199. Hacker, p. 583.

200. Bernhard, p. 18.

201. DeGregorio, s.v. "George Washington" (pp. 8-9).

202. Seabrook, EYWTAASIW, p. 521.

203. Seabrook, EYWTAASIW, p. 521.

204. Seabrook, EYWTAASIW, pp. 268, 525.

205. Simpson, pp. 69, 74.

206. Coit, pp. 170, 175.

207. Rozwenc, p. 50.

208. Seabrook, EYWTAASIW, p. 533. Let us note here that the U.S. is not a "democracy" and never has been: as this was not the intention of the Founders, the word appears nowhere in our 18th- or 19th-Century official government documents. Because it aligns with left-wing ideology, however, early liberal-minded enemies of confederation began pushing the false idea that "the U.S. is a democracy" on the public. Continually reinforced into modern times, it is held by many Americans into the present day, with even many liberal mainstream historians still referring to the U.S. as a "democratic republic" (see e.g., Smelser, TDR). The U.S., however, remains a republic (a government based on law) rather than a democracy (a government based on majority rule), despite the misleading moniker "Democrats" and the blatant attempts by the Left to rewrite history and trick the public.

209. For more on this topic see Seabrook, TQJD, passim; Seabrook, TAHSR, passim; Seabrook, TQAHS, passim.

210. For more on this particular subject see my books on Lincoln's War, in particular, *Everything You Were Taught About the Civil War is Wrong, Ask a Southerner!*

211. See D. S. Rowland, passim.

212. A Man of No Party, p. 10.

213. Tocqueville, p. 169.

214. Hamilton, Madison, and Jay, p. 89. See also M. D. Peterson, JM, pp. 102-103; Hacker, p. 213.

215. Seabrook, EYWTATCWIW, p. 32.

216. Stephens, Vol. 1, pp. 157-158.

217. J. Davis, RFCG, Vol. 2, pp. 621, 622. Only a dictator can issue laws overturning constitutional rights. See Crocker, p. 59.

218. Mitgang, pp. 403, 404; L. Johnson, pp. 123-124; Meriwether, p. 157; Horn, IE, p. 217.

219. Seabrook, AL, p. 291.

220. Neely, pp. 109-112.

221. See e.g., J. Davis, RFCG, Vol. 2, pp. 632-633; C. Johnson, p. 157; Lott, pp. 158-159; L. Johnson, p. 188; Grissom, pp. 115-116; Christian, p. 15; Cisco, passim; Grimsley, passim.

222. C. Adams, pp. 117-118.

223. "My policy is to have no policy," our crafty sixteenth president once said. Nicolay and Hay, ALAH, Vol. 4, p. 76.

224. D. H. Donald, WNWCW, pp. 84-88; Simmons, s.v. "Civil rights in the Confederacy"; L. Johnson, p. 176; Current, TC, s.v. "Davis, Jefferson."

225. See McCarty, passim.

226. For more on the original U.S. Confederacy, see Seabrook, AL, passim.

227. Seabrook, TQREL, p. 173.

228. See Seabrook, TCOTCSOA, passim.

229. Seabrook, AL, p. 90.

230. Seabrook, AL, p. 45.

231. Tocqueville, p. 169. Emphasis added.

232. Seabrook, EYWTATCWIW, p. 32.

233. Seabrook, EYWTATCWIW, pp. 112-113.

234. Seabrook, EYWTATCWIW, p. 31.

235. Seabrook, EYWTAASIW, pp. 459-514. See also Seabrook, S101, passim.

236. Seabrook, EYWTAASIW, pp. 647-685.

237. Seabrook, EYWTAASIW, pp. 445-458.

238. Seabrook, AL, p. 220.

239. Seabrook, EYWTAASIW, pp. 282-399.

240. Seabrook, EYWTAASIW, pp. 251-281.

241. Seabrook, EYWTAASIW, pp. 167-229.

242. Seabrook, EYWTAASIW, pp. 167-229.

243. See Seabrook, TGYC, passim.

244. Seabrook, EYWTAASIW, p. 575.

245. Seabrook, EYWTAASIW, p. 241.

246. Seabrook, EYWTAASIW, pp. 549-646.

247. Seabrook, TQREL, p. 106.

248. Seabrook, EYWTAASIW, pp. 799-800.

249. Kautz, p. 11.

250. Seabrook, EYWTATCWIW, pp. 158-159.

251. Seabrook, ARB, p. 259.

252. Eaton, HSC, p. 93.

253. Barrow, Segars, and Rosenburg, BC, p. 97; Hinkle, p. 106; *The United Daughters of the Confederacy Magazine*, Vols. 54-55, 1991, p. 32. If we utilize Yankee General August Valentine Kautz's definition of a "soldier," then as many as 1 million Southern blacks served in one capacity or another in the Confederate military. See Kautz, p. 11.

254. Hinkle, p. 108. See also Quintero, Gonzales, and Velazquez, passim.

255. Lonn, p. 218.

256. Rosen, p. 161.

257. Hinkle, p. 108; Blackerby, passim.

258. Seabrook, AL, p. 343.

259. P. J. Buchanan, p. 131.

260. L. Johnson, p. 150.

261. D. H. Donald, WNWCW, pp. 59-62.

262. Encyc. Brit., s.v. "Lincoln, Abraham"; Owsley, pp. 63-64; Hacker, p. 582.

263. DeGregorio, s.v. "John Quincy Adams." See also Vanauken, passim.

264. For examples of Lincoln's various dire warnings, threats, and promises to wage war on any European nation that impeded his illegal assault on the South, see Owsley, pp. 309, 315, 331, 350, 359, 399, 401, 402, 408, 411, 423, 425, 436, 440, 446, 453, 464, 507, 510, 516-517, 524, 539-540, 544.

265. Matthew 22:36-40; John 13:34; 15:17; 1 John 4:8, 16.

266. Seabrook, EYWTATCWIW, pp. 199-202.

267. Seabrook, AL, p. 530. My paraphrasal.

268. Tourgee, p. 300.

269. See Seabrook, EYWTATCWIW, pp. 203-209.

270. Montesquieu, Vol. 1, pp. 183-187.

BIBLIOGRAPHY

Adams, Charles. *When in the Course of Human Events: Arguing the Case for Southern Secession.* Lanham, MD: Rowman and Littlefield, 2000.

Adams, Charles Francis (ed.). *The Works of John Adams, Second President of the United States.* 10 vols. Boston, MA: Little, Brown and Co., 1853.

Adams, Henry (ed.). *Documents Relating to New-England Federalism, 1800-1815.* Boston, MA: Little, Brown, and Co., 1877.

Adams, John Quincy. *The New England Confederacy of 1643.* A Speech delivered May 29, 1843. Boston, MA: Charles C. Little and James Brown, 1843.

A Man of No Title (anonymous). *The Recovery of America Demonstrated to be Practicable by Great Britain, Upon Principles and Deductions that are Clear, Precise, and Convincing.* London, UK: G. Wilkie, 1782.

Ashe, Captain Samuel A'Court. *A Southern View of the Invasion of the Southern States and War of 1861-1865.* 1935. Crawfordville, GA: Ruffin Flag Co., 1938 ed.

Banks, Noreen. *Early American Almanac.* New York, NY: Bantam, 1975.

Barrow, Charles Kelly, J. H. Segars, and R. B. Rosenburg (eds.). *Black Confederates.* 1995. Gretna, LA: Pelican Publishing Co., 2001 ed.

Beach, Frederick Converse (ed.). *The Encyclopedia Americana.* 16 vols. New York, NY: The Americana Company, 1904.

Benson, Al, Jr., and Walter Donald Kennedy. *Lincoln's Marxists.* Gretna, LA: Pelican Publishing Co., 2011.

Bergh, Albert Ellery (ed.). *The Writings of Thomas Jefferson.* 20 vols. Washington, D.C.: Thomas Jefferson Memorial Association of the U.S., 1905.

Bernhard, Winfred E. A. (ed.). *Political Parties in American History - Vol. 1: 1789-1828.* New York, NY: G. P. Putnams' Sons, 1973.

Blackerby, Hubert R. *Blacks in Blue and Gray.* New Orleans, LA: Portals Press, 1979.

Boatner, Mark Mayo. *The Civil War Dictionary.* 1959. New York, NY: David McKay Co., 1988 ed.

Brooks, Elbridge Streeter. *The Story of the American Indian: His Origin, Development, Decline and Destiny.* Boston, MA: D. Lothrop Co., 1887.

Buchanan, Patrick J. *A Republic, Not an Empire: Reclaiming America's Destiny.* Washington, D.C.: Regenry, 1999.

Burns, James MacGregor, and Jack Walter Peltason. *Government by the People: The Dynamics of American National, State, and Local Government.* 1952. Englewood Cliffs, NJ: Prentice-Hall, 1964 ed.

Channing, Steven A. *Confederate Ordeal: The Southern Home Front.* 1984. Morristown, NJ: Time-Life Books, 1989 ed.

Christian, George L. *Abraham Lincoln: An Address Delivered Before R. E. Lee Camp, No. 1 Confederate Veterans at Richmond, VA, October 29, 1909.* Richmond, VA: L. H. Jenkins, 1909.

Cisco, Walter Brian. *War Crimes Against Southern Civilians.* Gretna, LA: Pelican Publishing Co., 2007.

Coit, Margaret L. *John C. Calhoun: American Portrait.* Boston, MA: Sentry, 1950.

Collier, Christopher, and James Lincoln Collier. *Decision in Philadelphia: The Constitutional Convention of 1787.* 1986. New York, NY: Ballantine, 1987 ed.

Compton's Pictured Encyclopedia and Fact-Index. 1922. Chicago, IL: F. E. Compton and Co., 1957 ed.

Cooke, Alistair. *Alistair Cooke's America.* 1973. New York, NY: Alfred A. Knopf, 1984 ed.

Crallé, Richard Kenner. (ed.). *The Works of John C. Calhoun.* 6 vols. New York: NY: D. Appleton and Co., 1853-1888.

Crocker, H. W., III. *The Politically Incorrect Guide to the Civil War.* Washington, D.C.: Regnery,

2008.

Current, Richard N. *The Lincoln Nobody Knows*. 1958. New York, NY: Hill and Wang, 1963 ed.

——. (ed.) *The Confederacy (Information Now Encyclopedia)*. 1993. New York, NY: Macmillan, 1998 ed.

Davis, Jefferson. *The Rise and Fall of the Confederate Government*. 2 vols. New York, NY: D. Appleton and Co., 1881.

——. *A Short History of the Confederate States of America*. New York, NY: Belford, 1890.

Davis, William C. *Jefferson Davis: The Man and His Hour*. New York, NY: HarperCollins, 1991.

DeGregorio, William A. *The Complete Book of U.S. Presidents*. 1984. New York, NY: Barricade, 1993 ed.

DiLorenzo, Thomas J. *The Real Lincoln: A New Look at Abraham Lincoln, His Agenda, and an Unnecessary War*. Three Rivers, MI: Three Rivers Press, 2003.

——. *Lincoln Unmasked: What You're Not Supposed to Know About Dishonest Abe*. New York, NY: Crown Forum, 2006.

Donald, David Herbert. *Lincoln Reconsidered: Essays on the Civil War Era*. 1947. New York, NY: Vintage Press, 1989 ed.

——. (ed.). *Why the North Won the Civil War*. 1960. New York, NY: Collier, 1962 ed.

Eaton, Clement. *A History of the Southern Confederacy*. 1945. New York, NY: Free Press, 1966 ed.

Elliot, Jonathan (ed.). *The Debates of the Several State Conventions, On the Adoption of the Federal Constitution, As Recommended by the General Convention at Philadelphia in 1787*. 5 vols. Washington, D.C.: Jonathan Elliot, 1836.

Encyclopedia Britannica: A New Survey of Universal Knowledge. 1768. Chicago, IL/London, UK: Encyclopedia Britannica, 1955 ed.

Evans, Clement A. (ed.). *Confederate Military History*. 12 vols. Atlanta, GA: Confederate Publishing Co., 1899.

Findlay, Bruce, and Esther Findlay. *Your Rugged Constitution: How America's House of Freedom is Planned and Built*. 1950. Stanford, CA: Stanford University Press, 1951 ed.

Foley, John P. (ed.). *The Jeffersonian Cyclopedia*. New York, NY: Funk and Wagnalls, 1900.

Forman, S. E. *The Life and Writings of Thomas Jefferson*. Indianapolis, IN: Bowen-Merrill, 1900.

Gales, Joseph, and William W. Seaton (eds.). *Register of Debates in Congress, Comprising the Leading Debates and Incidents of the Second Session of the Twenty-Second Congress* (Vol. 9). Washington, D.C.: Gales and Seaton, 1833.

Garland, Hugh A. *The Life of John Randolph of Roanoke*. New York, NY: D. Appleton and Co., 1874.

Grimsley, Mark. *The Hard Hand of War: Union Military Policy Toward Southern Civilians, 1861-1865*. 1995. Cambridge, UK: Cambridge University Press, 1997 ed.

Grissom, Michael Andrew. *Southern By the Grace of God*. 1988. Gretna, LA: Pelican Publishing Co., 1995 ed.

Hacker, Louis Morton. *The Shaping of the American Tradition*. New York, NY: Columbia University Press, 1947.

Hamilton, Alexander, James Madison, and John Jay. *The Federalist: A Collection of Essays by Alexander Hamilton, James Madison, and John Jay*. New York, NY: The Co-operative Publication Society, 1901.

Hamilton, Stanislaus Murray (ed.). *The Writings of James Monroe* (Vol. 1, 1778-1794). N.p., 1794.

Hamilton, William. *The Life, Surprising Adventures and Heroic Actions of Sir William Wallace, General and Governor of Scotland*. Edinburgh, Scotland: Robert Clark, 1770.

Henry, Robert Selph (ed.). *The Story of the Confederacy*. 1931. New York, NY: Konecky and Konecky, 1999 ed.

Hinkle, Don. *Embattled Banner: A Reasonable Defense of the Confederate Battle Flag*. Paducah, KY: Turner Publishing Co., 1997.

Hodge, Frederick Webb. *Handbook of American Indians North of Mexico*. 2 vols. Washington, D.C.: Government Printing Office, 1907.

Horn, Stanley F. *Invisible Empire: The Story of the Ku Klux Klan, 1866-1871*. 1939. Montclair, NJ: Patterson Smith, 1969 ed.

Jensen, Merrill. *The New Nation: A History of the United States During the Confederation, 1781-1789*. New York, NY: Vintage, 1950.

———. *The Articles of Confederation: An Interpretation of the Social-Constitutional History of the American Revolution, 1774-1781*. Madison, WI: University of Wisconsin Press, 1959.

Johnson, Clint. *The Politically Incorrect Guide to the South (and Why It Will Rise Again)*. Washington, D.C.: Regnery, 2006.

Johnson, Ludwell H. *North Against South: The American Iliad, 1848-1877*. 1978. Columbia, SC: Foundation for American Education, 1993 ed.

Jones, John B. *A Rebel War Clerk's Diary at the Confederate States Capital*. 2 vols. Philadelphia, PA: J. B. Lippencott and Co., 1866.

Journal of the Congress of the Confederate States of America, 1861-1865. 7 vols. Washington, D.C.: Government Printing Office, 1904-1905.

Kautz, August Valentine. *Customs of Service for Non-Commissioned Officers and Soldiers (as Derived from Law and Regulations and Practised in the Army of the United States)*. Philadelphia, PA: J. B. Lippincott and Co., 1864.

King, Charles R. (ed.). *The Life and Correspondence of Rufus King*. 6 vols. New York, NY: G. P. Putnam's Sons, 1897.

Knight, Charles (ed.). *London*. 6 vols. London, UK: Charles Knight and Co., 1843.

Litwack, Leon F. *North of Slavery: The Negro in the Free States, 1790-1860*. Chicago, IL: University of Chicago Press, 1961.

———. *Been in the Storm So Long: The Aftermath of Slavery*. New York, NY: Vintage, 1980.

Lonn, Ella. *Foreigners in the Confederacy*. 1940. Chapel Hill, NC: University of North Carolina Press, 2002 ed.

Lott, Stanley K. *The Truth About American Slavery*. 2004. Clearwater, SC: Eastern Digital Resources, 2005 ed.

Madison, James. *The Papers of James Madison* (Congressional Series). 17 vols. New York, NY: J. and H. G. Langley, 1841.

Main, Jackson Turner. *The Anti-Federalists: Critics of the Constitution, 1781-1788*. 1961. New York, NY: W. W. Norton and Co., 1974 ed.

Marshall, James V. *The United States Manual of Biography and History*. Philadelphia, PA: James B. Smith and Co., 1856.

McCarty, Burke (ed.). *Little Sermons In Socialism by Abraham Lincoln*. Chicago, IL: The Chicago Daily Socialist, 1910.

McPherson, Edward. *The Political History of the United States of America, During the Great Rebellion (From November 6, 1860, to July 4, 1864)*. Washington, D.C.: Philp and Solomons, 1864.

———. *The Political History of the United States of America, During the Period of Reconstruction, (From April 15, 1865, to July 15, 1870,) Including a Classified Summary of the Legislation of the Thirty-ninth, Fortieth, and Forty-first Congresses*. Washington, D.C.: Solomons and Chapman, 1875.

Meriwether, Elizabeth Avery. *Facts and Falsehoods Concerning the War on the South, 1861-1865*. (Originally written under the pseudonym "George Edmonds.") Memphis, TN: A. R. Taylor, 1904.

Mitgang, Herbert (ed.). *Lincoln As They Saw Him*. 1956. New York, NY: Collier, 1962 ed.

Montesquieu, Baron de. *The Spirit of Laws* (Vol. 1). London, UK: J. Nourse and P. Vaillant, 1750.

Moore, Frank (ed.). *The Rebellion Record: A Diary of American Events*. 12 vols. New York, NY: G. P. Putnam, 1861.

Napolitano, Andrew P. *The Constitution in Exile: How the Federal Government has Seized Power by Rewriting the Supreme Law of the Land.* Nashville, TN: Nelson Current, 2006.

Neely, Mark E., Jr. *The Fate of Liberty: Abraham Lincoln and Civil Liberties.* New York, NY: Oxford University Press, 1991.

Nicolay, John G., and John Hay (eds.). *Abraham Lincoln: A History.* 10 vols. New York, NY: The Century Co., 1890.

——. *Complete Works of Abraham Lincoln.* 12 vols. 1894. New York, NY: Francis D. Tandy Co., 1905 ed.

——. *Abraham Lincoln: Complete Works.* 12 vols. 1894. New York, NY: The Century Co., 1907 ed.

Nivola, Pietro S., and David H. Rosenbloom (eds.). *Classic Readings in American Politics.* New York, NY: St. Martin's Press, 1986.

O'Brien, Cormac. *Secret Lives of the U.S. Presidents: What Your Teachers Never Told You About the Men of the White House.* Philadelphia, PA: Quirk, 2004.

——. *Secret Lives of the Civil War: What Your teachers Never Told You About the War Between the States.* Philadelphia, PA: Quirk, 2007.

ORA (full title: *The War of the Rebellion: A Compilation of the Official Records of the Union and Confederate Armies.* (Multiple volumes.) Washington, D.C.: Government Printing Office, 1880.

ORN (full title: *Official Records of the Union and Confederate Navies in the War of the Rebellion*). (Multiple volumes.) Washington, D.C.: Government Printing Office, 1894.

Owsley, Frank Lawrence. *King Cotton Diplomacy: Foreign Relations of the Confederate States of America.* 1931. Chicago, IL: University of Chicago Press, 1959 ed.

Peterson, Merrill D. (ed.). *James Madison, A Biography in His Own Words.* (First published posthumously in 1840.) New York, NY: Harper and Row, 1974 ed.

——. (ed.). *Thomas Jefferson: Writings, Autobiography, A Summary View of the Rights of British America, Notes on the State of Virginia, Public Papers, Addresses, Messages and Replies, Miscellany, Letters.* New York, NY: Literary Classics, 1984.

Pollard, Edward A. *Southern History of the War.* 2 vols. in 1. New York, NY: Charles B. Richardson, 1866.

——. *The Lost Cause.* 1867. Chicago, IL: E. B. Treat, 1890 ed.

——. *The Lost Cause Regained.* New York, NY: G. W. Carlton and Co., 1868.

——. *Life of Jefferson Davis, With a Secret History of the Southern Confederacy, Gathered "Behind the Scenes in Richmond."* Philadelphia, PA: National Publishing Co., 1869.

Quintero, José Agustín, Ambrosio José Gonzales, and Loreta Janeta Velazquez (Phillip Thomas Tucker, ed.). *Cubans in the Confederacy.* Jefferson, NC: McFarland and Co., 2002.

Randolph, Thomas Jefferson (ed.). *Memoir, Correspondence, and Miscellanies, from the Papers of Thomas Jefferson.* 4 vols. Charlottesville, VA: F. Carr and Co., 1829.

Ransom, Roger L. *Conflict and Compromise: The Political Economy of Slavery, Emancipation, and the American Civil War.* Cambridge, UK: Cambridge University Press, 1989.

Rawle, William. *A View of the Constitution of the United States of America.* Philadelphia, PA: Philip H. Nicklin, 1829.

Richardson, John Anderson. *Richardson's Defense of the South.* Atlanta, GA: A. B. Caldwell, 1914.

Rosen, Robert N. *The Jewish Confederates.* Columbia, SC: University of South Carolina Press, 2000.

Rosenbaum, Robert A., and Douglas Brinkley (eds.). *The Penguin Encyclopedia of American History.* New York, NY: Viking, 2003.

Rouse, Adelaide Louise (ed.). *National Documents: State Papers So Arranged as to Illustrate the Growth of Our Country From 1606 to the Present Day.* New York, NY: Unit Book Publishing Co., 1906.

Rowland, David S. *Historical Remarks, With Moral Reflections.* Providence, RI: John Carter, 1779.

Rowland, Dunbar (ed.). *Jefferson Davis, Constitutionalist: His Letters, Papers, and Speeches.* 10 vols.

Jackson, MS: Mississippi Department of Archives and History, 1923.

Rozwenc, Edwin Charles (ed.). *The Causes of the American Civil War*. 1961. Lexington, MA: D. C. Heath and Co., 1972 ed.

Seabrook, Lochlainn. *Carnton Plantation Ghost Stories: True Tales of the Unexplained From Tennessee's Most Haunted Civil War House!* 2005. Franklin, TN: Sea Raven Press, 2010 ed.

——. *Nathan Bedford Forrest: Southern Hero, American Patriot: Honoring a Confederate Hero and the Old South*. 2007. Franklin, TN: Sea Raven Press, 2010 ed.

——. *Abraham Lincoln: The Southern View*. 2007. Franklin, TN: Sea Raven Press, 2013 ed.

——. *The McGavocks of Carnton Plantation: A Southern History - Celebrating One of Dixie's Most Noble Confederate Families and Their Tennessee Home*. 2008. Franklin, TN: Sea Raven Press, 2011 ed.

——. *A Rebel Born: A Defense of Nathan Bedford Forrest*. 2010. Franklin, TN: Sea Raven Press, 2011 ed.

——. *A Rebel Born: The Movie* (screenplay). Franklin, TN: Sea Raven Press, unpublished.

——. *Everything You Were Taught About the Civil War is Wrong, Ask a Southerner!* 2010. Franklin, TN: Sea Raven Press, revised 2014 ed.

——. *The Quotable Jefferson Davis: Selections From the Writings and Speeches of the Confederacy's First President*. Franklin, TN: Sea Raven Press, 2011.

——. *Lincolnology: The Real Abraham Lincoln Revealed In His Own Words*. Franklin, TN: Sea Raven Press, 2011.

——. *The Unquotable Abraham Lincoln: The President's Quotes They Don't Want You To Know!* Franklin, TN: Sea Raven Press, 2011.

——. *The Quotable Robert E. Lee: Selections From the Writings and Speeches of the South's Most Beloved Civil War General*. 2011. Franklin, TN: Sea Raven Press, 2014 ed.

——. *The Constitution of the Confederate States of America Explained: A Clause-by-Clause Study of the South's Magna Carta*. Franklin, TN: Sea Raven Press, 2012.

——. *The Old Rebel: Robert E. Lee As He Was Seen By His Contemporaries*. Franklin, TN: Sea Raven Press, 2012.

——. *The Quotable Stonewall Jackson: Selections From the Writings and Speeches of the South's Most Famous General*. Franklin, TN: Sea Raven Press, 2012.

——. *Honest Jeff and Dishonest Abe: A Southern Children's Guide to the Civil War*. Franklin, TN: Sea Raven Press, 2012.

——. *Give 'Em Hell Boys! The Complete Military Correspondence of Nathan Bedford Forrest*. Franklin, TN: Sea Raven Press, 2012 Sesquicentennial Civil War Edition.

——. *The Great Impersonator: 99 Reasons to Dislike Abraham Lincoln*. Franklin, TN: Sea Raven Press, 2012.

——. *Forrest! 99 Reasons to Love Nathan Bedford Forrest*. Franklin, TN: Sea Raven Press, 2012 Sesquicentennial Civil War Edition.

——. *The Quotable Nathan Bedford Forrest: Selections From the Writings and Speeches of the Confederacy's Most Brilliant Cavalryman*. Franklin, TN: Sea Raven Press, 2012 Sesquicentennial Civil War Edition.

——. *Encyclopedia of the Battle of Franklin: A Comprehensive Guide to the Conflict That Changed the Civil War*. Franklin, TN: Sea Raven Press, 2012 Sesquicentennial Civil War Edition.

——. *The Quotable Alexander H. Stephens: Selections From the Writings and Speeches of the Confederacy's First Vice President*. Franklin, TN: Sea Raven Press, 2013.

——. *The Alexander H. Stephens Reader: Excerpts From the Works of a Confederate Founding Father*. Franklin, TN: Sea Raven Press, 2013.

——. *Saddle, Sword, and Gun: A Biography of Nathan Bedford Forrest For Teens*. Franklin, TN: Sea Raven Press, 2013 Sesquicentennial Civil War Edition.

——. *The Articles of Confederation Explained: A Clause-by-Clause Study of America's First Constitution*.

Franklin, TN: Sea Raven Press, 2014.

——. *Give This Book to a Yankee: A Southern Guide to the Civil War For Northerners.* Franklin, TN: Sea Raven Press, 2014.

——. *American Slavery 101: Amazing Facts You Never Knew About America's "Peculiar Institution."* Franklin, TN: Sea Raven Press, 2015.

——. *The Great Yankee Coverup: What the North Doesn't Want You to Know About Lincoln's War!* Franklin, TN: Sea Raven Press, 2015.

——. *Confederate Blood and Treasure: An Interview With Lochlainn Seabrook.* Franklin, TN: Sea Raven Press, 2015.

——. *Confederate Flag Facts.* Franklin, TN: Sea Raven Press, 2015.

Shorto, Russell. *Thomas Jefferson and the American Ideal.* Hauppauge, NY: Barron's, 1987.

Simpson, Lewis P. (ed.). *I'll Take My Stand: The South and the Agrarian Tradition.* 1930. Baton Rouge, LA: University of Louisiana Press, 1977 ed.

Smelser, Marshall. *American Colonial and Revolutionary History.* 1950. New York, NY: Barnes and Noble, 1966 ed.

——. *The Democratic Republic, 1801-1815.* New York, NY: Harper and Row, 1968.

Smith, Robert. *The Obligations of the Confederate States of North America to Praise God.* Philadelphia, PA: Robert Smith, 1782.

Stephens, Alexander H. *A Constitutional View of the Late War Between the States.* 2 vols. Philadelphia, PA: National Publishing Co., 1868.

Tocqueville, Alexis de. *Democracy in America.* 1 vol. ed. New York, NY: Pratt, Woodford, and Co., 1848.

Tourgee, Albion W. *A Fool's Errand By One of the Fools.* London, UK: George Routledge and Sons, 1883.

Tyler, Lyon Gardiner. *The Letters and Times of the Tylers.* 3 vols. Williamsburg, VA: N.P., 1896.

——. *Propaganda in History.* Richmond, VA: Richmond Press, 1920.

——. *The Gray Book: A Confederate Catechism.* Columbia, TN: Gray Book Committee, SCV, 1935.

Upshur, Abel Parker. *A Brief Enquiry Into the True Nature and Character of Our Federal Government.* Philadelphia, PA: John Campbell, 1863.

Vanauken, Sheldon. *The Glittering Illusion: English Sympathy for the Southern Confederacy.* Washington, D.C.: Regnery, 1989.

Victor, Orville James. *The History, Civil, Political, and Military, of the Southern Rebellion, From its Incipient Stages to its Close* (Vol. 3). New York, NY: James D. Torrey, 1861.

——. *The Comprehensive History of the Southern Rebellion and the War for the Union* (Vol. 1.) New York, NY: James D. Torrey, 1862.

Washington, Henry Augustine. *The Writings of Thomas Jefferson.* 9 vols. New York, NY: H. W. Derby, 1861.

Weintraub, Max. *The Blue Book of American History.* New York, NY: Regents Publishing Co., 1960.

Williams, Edwin (ed.). *Presidents' Messages: Inaugural, Annual and Special, From 1789 to 1846* (Vol. 2). New York, NY: Edward Walker, 1846.

Wood, Robert C. *Confederate Hand-Book: A Compilation of Important Data and Other Interesting and Valuable Matter Relating to the War Between the States, 1861-1865.* New Orleans, LA: L. Graham and Son, 1900.

Woods, Thomas E., Jr. *The Politically Incorrect Guide to American History.* Washington, D.C.: Regnery, 2004.

INDEX

Adams, John, 26, 46, 69
Adams, John Quincy, 45
Adams, Samuel, 27, 32, 69
Adams, Shelby L., 126
Anderson, Loni, 126
Andrew, Saint, 104
Arthur, King, 125
Atkins, Chet, 126
Barnett, T. J., 105
Bartlett, Josiah, 68
Beauregard, Pierre G. T., 126
Bellamy, Francis, 86
Benjamin, Judah P., 100
Benton, Thomas Hart, 33
Bernstein, Leonard, 126
Bolling, Edith, 126
Boone, Daniel, 126
Boone, Pat, 126
Boudinot, Elias, 24
Braxton, Carter, 69
Breckinridge, John C., 126
Brooke, Edward W., 126
Brooks, Elbridge S., 13
Brooks, Preston S., 126
Buchanan, James, 51-53
Buchanan, Patrick J., 126
Buford, Abraham, 126
Burke, Thomas, 87
Burr, Aaron, 47
Butler, Andrew P., 126
Calhoun, John C., 87
Campbell, Joseph, 125
Carroll, Charles (of Carrollton), 69
Carson, Martha, 126
Carter, Theodrick "Tod", 126
Cash, Johnny, 126
Cass, Lewis, 35
Caudill, Benjamin E., 125
Chase, Samuel, 69
Cheairs, Nathaniel F., 126
Chesnut, Mary, 126
Clark, Abraham, 69

Clark, William, 126
Clay, Henry, 85, 87, 88
Clymer, George, 69
Cobb, Howell, 73, 77
Combs, Bertram T., 126
Crawford, Cindy, 126
Crawford, William, 63
Crockett, Davy, 126
Cruise, Tom, 126
Cyrus, Billy R., 126
Cyrus, Miley, 126
Davis, Jefferson, 8, 34, 41, 51, 60,
    63, 67, 76, 79, 89, 92, 97,
    125, 126
Douglas, Stephen A., 35, 36
Duvall, Robert, 126
Edward I, King, 107, 125
Ellery, William, 69
Floyd, William, 69
Foote, Shelby, 125
Forbes, Christopher, 126
Forrest, Nathan B., 8, 101, 125, 126
Franklin, Benjamin, 25, 58, 69
Gayheart, Rebecca, 126
George III, King, 65-67, 106
George, Saint, 104
Gerry, Elbridge, 69
Gist, States R., 126
Gordon, George W., 126
Gorham, Nathaniel, 24
Grant, Ulysses S., 84, 93, 94
Graves, Robert, 125
Griffin, Cyrus, 24
Guaraldi, Vince, 126
Gwinnett, Button, 69
Hall, Lyman, 69
Hamilton, Alexander, 12, 14, 18, 27,
    32, 85, 86, 88, 90
Hamilton, James, Jr., 38
Hamlin, Hannibal, 72
Hancock, John, 24, 27
Hanson, John, 24

Harding, William G., 126
Harrison, Benjamin, 69
Harrison, William H., 33
Hart, John, 69
Hayes, Rutherford B., 105
Henry, Patrick, 27-30
Hewes, Joseph, 69
Heyward, Thomas, Jr., 69
Hitler, Adolf, 86
Hood, John B., 126
Hooper, William, 69
Hopkins, Stephen, 69
Hopkinson, Francis, 69
Huntington, Samuel, 23, 69
Jackson, Andrew, 38, 126
Jackson, Henry R., 126
Jackson, Thomas "Stonewall", 126
James, Frank, 126
James, Jesse, 126
Jay, John, 17, 27, 32, 65
Jefferson, Thomas, 13, 15, 19, 27,
        33, 34, 46, 47, 50, 63-67,
        69, 76, 86, 87, 90, 91, 93,
        104, 107, 126
Jent, Elias, Sr., 125
Jesus, 104, 125
John, Elton, 126
Johnston, Joseph E., 8
Judd, Ashley, 126
Judd, Naomi, 126
Judd, Wynonna, 126
Kautz, August V., 101
Kenner, Duncan F., 100
King, Rufus, 47
Lee, Fitzhugh, 126
Lee, Francis Lightfoot, 69
Lee, Richard Henry, 24, 27, 69
Lee, Robert E., 67, 81, 92, 93, 100,
        126
Lee, Stephen D., 126
Lee, William H. F., 126
Leonidas, King, 106
Lewis, Francis, 69
Lewis, Meriwether, 126

Lincoln, Abraham, 8, 31, 35, 36,
        51-56, 64-66, 71, 72, 76,
        78, 79, 82, 85-90, 92, 100,
        101, 103, 105-107
Livingston, Philip, 69
Longstreet, James, 126
Loveless, Patty, 126
Lynch, Thomas, Jr., 69
Madison, James, 15, 32, 39, 49, 52,
        64, 91
Manigault, Arthur M., 126
Manigault, Joseph, 126
Marshall, James V., 44
Marvin, Lee, 126
Maury, Abram P., 126
McCarty, Burke, 86
McGavock, Caroline E. (Winder),
        126
McGavock, David H., 126
McGavock, Emily, 126
McGavock, Francis, 126
McGavock, James R., 126
McGavock, John W., 126
McGavock, Lysander, 126
McGavock, Randal W., 126
McGraw, Tim, 126
McKean, Thomas, 24, 69
Meriwether, Elizabeth A., 126
Meriwether, Minor, 126
Middleton, Arthur, 69
Mifflin, Thomas, 24
Monroe, James, 32, 46
Montesquieu, Baron de, 15, 108
Morgan, John H., 126
Morris, Lewis, 69
Morris, Robert, 69
Morton, John, 69
Morton, John W., 126
Mosby, John S., 126
Nelson, Louis Napoleon, 101
Nelson, Thomas, Jr., 69
Nugent, Ted, 126
Paca, William, 69
Paine, Robert Treat, 69

Parton, Dolly, 126
Patrick, Saint, 104
Penn, John, 69
Pettus, Edmund W., 126
Phillips, Samuel, 38
Pickering, Timothy, 46, 47, 50
Pierce, Franklin, 35
Pillow, Gideon J., 126
Pinckney, Thomas, 38
Polk, James K., 34, 126
Polk, Leonidas, 126
Polk, Lucius E., 126
Presley, Elvis, 126
Randolph, Edmund J., 126
Randolph, George W., 126
Randolph, John, 67
Ravensdale, Cassidy, 4
Rawle, William, 61
Read, George, 69
Reagan, Ronald, 126
Reynolds, Burt, 126
Robbins, Hargus, 126
Robert the Bruce, King, 125
Rodney, Caesar, 69
Ross, Betsy, 75
Ross, George, 69
Rowland, David S., 39, 91
Rucker, Edmund W., 126
Rush, Benjamin, 69
Rutledge, Edward, 69
Scruggs, Earl, 126
Seabrook, John L., 126
Seabrook, Lochlainn, 4, 125-127
Seger, Bob, 126
Seward, William H., 103
Sherman, Roger, 69
Skaggs, Ricky, 126
Smith, James, 69
St. Clair, Arthur, 24
Stephens, Alexander H., 8, 41, 42,
        80, 90, 126
Stewart, Alexander P., 126
Stockton, Richard, 69
Stone, Thomas, 69

Stuart, Jeb, 126
Taylor, George, 69
Taylor, Richard, 8, 126
Taylor, Sarah K., 126
Taylor, Zachary, 126
Thornton, Matthew, 68
Tocqueville, Alexis de, 39, 40, 59,
        91, 93, 96, 107
Toombs, Robert A., 34
Tourgee, Albion W., 105, 106
Tucker, St. George, 93
Tyler, John, 33, 62
Tynes, Ellen B., 126
Upshur, Abel Parker, 62
Van Buren, Martin, 33
Vance, Robert B., 126
Vance, Zebulon, 126
Venable, Charles S., 126
Wallace, William, 107
Walton, George, 69
Washington, George, 23, 24, 30, 37,
        46, 76, 91
Washington, John A., 126
Washington, Thornton A., 126
Whipple, William, 68
Williams, William, 69
Wilson, James, 69
Wilson, Woodrow, 51, 126
Winbush, Nelson W., 101
Winder, Charles S., 126
Winder, John H., 126
Witherspoon, John, 69
Witherspoon, Reese, 126
Wolcott, Oliver, 69
Womack, John B., 126
Womack, Lee A., 126
Wythe, George, 69
Xerxes I, King, 106
Zollicoffer, Felix K., 126

MEET THE AUTHOR

OCHLAINN SEABROOK, winner of the prestigious Jefferson Davis Historical Gold Medal for his "masterpiece," *A Rebel Born: A Defense of Nathan Bedford Forrest*, is an unreconstructed Southern historian, award-winning author, Civil War scholar, and traditional Southern Agrarian of Scottish, English, Irish, Welsh, German, and Italian extraction. An encyclopedist, lexicographer, musician, artist, graphic designer, genealogist, and photographer, as well as an award-winning poet, songwriter, and screenwriter, he has a 40 year background in historical nonfiction writing and is a member of the Sons of Confederate Veterans, the Civil War Trust, and the National Grange.

Due to similarities in their writing styles, ideas, and literary works, Seabrook is often referred to as the "new Shelby Foote," the "Southern Joseph Campbell," and the "American Robert Graves" (his English cousin).

The grandson of an Appalachian coal-mining family, Seabrook is a seventh-generation Kentuckian, co-chair of the Jent/Gent Family Committee (Kentucky), founder and director of the Blakeney Family Tree Project, and a board member of the Friends of Colonel Benjamin E. Caudill.

COPYRIGHT ©
SEA RAVEN PRESS

Seabrook's literary works have been endorsed by leading authorities, museum curators, award-winning historians, bestselling authors, celebrities, noted scientists, well respected educators, TV show hosts and producers, renowned military artists, esteemed Southern organizations, and distinguished academicians from around the world.

Seabrook has authored over 40 popular adult books on the American Civil War, American and international slavery, the U.S. Confederacy (1781), the Southern Confederacy (1861), religion, theology and thealogy, Jesus, the Bible, the Apocrypha, the Law of Attraction, alternative health, spirituality, ghost stories, the paranormal, ufology, social issues, and cross-cultural studies of the family and marriage. His Confederate biographies, pro-South studies, genealogical monographs, family histories, military encyclopedias, self-help guides, and etymological dictionaries have received wide acclaim.

Seabrook's eight children's books include a Southern guide to the Civil War, a biography of Nathan Bedford Forrest, a dictionary of religion and myth, a rewriting of the King Arthur legend (which reinstates the original pre-Christian motifs), two bedtime stories for preschoolers, a naturalist's guidebook to owls, a worldwide look at the family, and an examination of the Near-Death Experience.

Of blue-blooded Southern stock through his Kentucky, Tennessee, Virginia, West Virginia, and North Carolina ancestors, he is a direct descendant of European royalty via his 6th great-grandfather, the Earl of Oxford, after which London's famous Harley Street is named. Among his celebrated male Celtic ancestors is Robert the Bruce, King of Scotland, Seabrook's 22nd great-grandfather. The 21st great-grandson of Edward I "Longshanks" Plantagenet), King of England, Seabrook is a thirteenth-generation Southerner through his descent from the colonists of Jamestown, Virginia (1607).

The 2nd, 3rd, and 4th great-grandson of dozens of Confederate soldiers, one of his closest connections to the War for Southern Independence is through his 3rd great-grandfather, Elias Jent, Sr., who fought for the Confederacy in the Thirteenth Cavalry Kentucky under Seabrook's 2nd cousin, Colonel Benjamin E. Caudill. The Thirteenth, also known as "Caudill's Army," fought in numerous conflicts, including the Battles of Saltville, Gladsville, Mill Cliff, Poor Fork, Whitesburg, and Leatherwood.

Seabrook is a descendant of the families of Alexander H. Stephens, John Singleton Mosby, and Edmund Winchester Rucker, and is related to the following Confederates and other 19th-Century luminaries: Robert E. Lee, Stephen Dill Lee, Stonewall Jackson, Nathan Bedford Forrest, James Longstreet, John Hunt Morgan, Jeb Stuart, P. G. T. Beauregard (designed the Confederate Battle Flag), George W. Gordon, John Bell Hood, Alexander Peter Stewart, Arthur M. Manigault, Joseph Manigault, Charles Scott Venable, Thornton A. Washington, John A.

Washington, Abraham Buford, Edmund W. Pettus, Theodrick "Tod" Carter, John B. Womack, John H. Winder, Gideon J. Pillow, States Rights Gist, Henry R. Jackson, John Lawton Seabrook, John C. Breckinridge, Leonidas Polk, Zachary Taylor, Sarah Knox Taylor (first wife of Jefferson Davis), Richard Taylor, Davy Crockett, Daniel Boone, Meriwether Lewis (of the Lewis and Clark Expedition) Andrew Jackson, James K. Polk, Abram Poindexter Maury (founder of Franklin, TN), William Giles Harding, Zebulon Vance, Thomas Jefferson, Edmund Jennings Randolph, George Wythe Randolph (grandson of Jefferson), Felix K. Zollicoffer, Fitzhugh Lee, Nathaniel F. Cheairs, Jesse James, Frank James, Robert Brank Vance, Charles Sidney Winder, John W. McGavock, Caroline E. (Winder) McGavock,

(Photo © Lochlainn Seabrook)

David Harding McGavock, Lysander McGavock, James Randal McGavock, Randal William McGavock, Francis McGavock, Emily McGavock, William Henry F. Lee, Lucius E. Polk, Minor Meriwether (husband of noted pro-South author Elizabeth Avery Meriwether), Ellen Bourne Tynes (wife of Forrest's chief of artillery, Captain John W. Morton), South Carolina Senators Preston Smith Brooks and Andrew Pickens Butler, and famed South Carolina diarist Mary Chesnut.

Seabrook's modern day cousins include: Patrick J. Buchanan (conservative author), Cindy Crawford (model), Shelby Lee Adams (Letcher County, Kentucky, portrait photographer), Bertram Thomas Combs (Kentucky's fiftieth governor), Edith Bolling (wife of President Woodrow Wilson), and actors Robert Duvall, Reese Witherspoon, Lee Marvin, Rebecca Gayheart, Andy Griffith, and Tom Cruise.

Seabrook's screenplay, A Rebel Born, based on his book of the same name, has been signed with acclaimed filmmaker Christopher Forbes (of Forbes Film). It is now in pre-production, and is set for release in 2016 as a full-length feature film. This will be the first movie ever made of Nathan Bedford Forrest's life story, and as a historically accurate project written from the Southern perspective, is destined to be one of the most talked about Civil War films of all time.

Born with music in his blood, Seabrook is an award-winning, multi-genre, BMI-Nashville songwriter and lyricist who has composed some 3,000 songs (250 albums), and whose original music has been heard in film (A Rebel Born, Union Bound, Cowgirls 'n Angels) and on TV and radio worldwide. A musician, producer, multi-instrumentalist, and renown performer—whose keyboard work has been variously compared to pianists from Hargus Robbins and Vince Guaraldi to Elton John and Leonard Bernstein—Seabrook has opened for groups such as the Earl Scruggs Review, Ted Nugent, and Bob Seger, and has performed privately for such public figures as President Ronald Reagan, Burt Reynolds, Loni Anderson, and Senator Edward W. Brooke. Seabrook's cousins in the music business include: Johnny Cash, Elvis Presley, Billy Ray and Miley Cyrus, Patty Loveless, Tim McGraw, Lee Ann Womack, Dolly Parton, Pat Boone, Naomi, Wynonna, and Ashley Judd, Ricky Skaggs, the Sunshine Sisters, Martha Carson, and Chet Atkins.

Seabrook lives with his wife and family in historic Middle Tennessee, the heart of Forrest country and the Confederacy, where his conservative Southern ancestors fought valiantly against Liberal Lincoln and the progressive North in defense of Jeffersonianism, constitutional government, and personal liberty.

If you enjoyed this book you will be interested in Mr. Seabrook's other popular Civil War related titles:

- THE CONSTITUTION OF THE CONFEDERATE STATES OF AMERICA EXPLAINED
- THE ARTICLES OF CONFEDERATION EXPLAINED
- EVERYTHING YOU WERE TAUGHT ABOUT THE CIVIL WAR IS WRONG, ASK A SOUTHERNER!
- EVERYTHING YOU WERE TAUGHT ABOUT AMERICAN SLAVERY IS WRONG, ASK A SOUTHERNER!

Available from Sea Raven Press and wherever fine books are sold

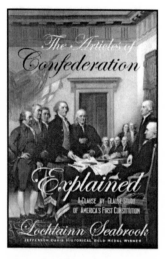
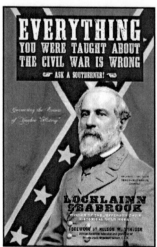
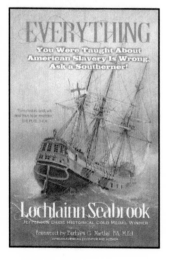

ALL OF OUR BOOK COVERS ARE AVAILABLE AS 11" X 17" POSTERS, SUITABLE FOR FRAMING.

SeaRavenPress.com

CPSIA information can be obtained at www.ICGtesting.com
Printed in the USA
LVOW08s0116011015

456461LV00001B/127/P